# KESEY

**Books by Ken Kesey**
available from The Viking Press, Inc., 625 Madison Avenue, New Yor
N.Y. 10022

One Flew Over the Cuckoo's Nest

One Flew Over the Cuckoo's Nest
(critical edition, edited by John Clark Pratt)

Sometimes A Great Notion

# KESEY

Edited by
Michael Strelow and the staff
of the Northwest Review

**NORTHWEST REVIEW BOOKS**
**Eugene, Oregon**

This book constitutes Volume XVI, Numbers
One and Two of the *Northwest Review.*
ISSN 0029-3423

Northwest Review Books edition, 1977
FIRST EDITION
Copyright © 1977 by Northwest Review Books

Library of Congress Cataloging in Publication Data

Kesey, Ken.
    Kesey.

    "This book constitutes volume xvi, numbers one and two of the
Northwest Review. ISSN 0029 3423."
    I. Strelow, Michael, 1943 -        II. Northwest Review, v. 16,
no. 1,2.
PS3561.E667A6        1977        813'.54        77-936
ISBN 0-918402-01-8
ISBN 0-918402-02-6 pbk.

## EDITOR'S NOTE

Ken Kesey as a phenomenon of the sixties became a metaphor of the American cultural experience in Tom Wolfe's book, **The Electric Kool-Aid Acid Test.** Kesey has said that Wolfe's record of the Merry Pranksters, the acid tests, the bus trips, the gatherings, was 96% accurate. And it is Kesey who has had to live with ideas of himself that coagulated in the public mind because of the popularity of Wolfe's book. Easily outlasting the images in Wolfe's exuberant prose have been the stories of Kesey's two major works, **One Flew Over the Cuckoo's Nest,** and **Sometimes a Great Notion.** Both became part of the public and scholarly consciousness, no matter what the movie versions were, by virtue of the fact that they were superior tales told in a superior way. Wolfe's book has been transformed by time from its original classification of "sociology" to what today might be called "recent history." And it is what Wolfe's book does not treat, Ken Kesey as a meticulous and accomplished writer, that is important now and for the future of American Literature.

Kesey is a good writer. He is one of a handful of American tale-makers whose work grows in stature. From newspaper headlines to sociological studies come affirmations that his imaginary vision of America is valuable as we try to learn to live in the twentieth century. This book is a record of Ken Kesey the writer and tries to document that rare process involved in telling good stories.

The sections from Kesey's new novel-in-progress (he calls it "form in transit") are the only parts of this book that Kesey preened and finished (and meant) for print. Much of the other material was never intended for publication. Consequently there appears a lot of playful and imaginative structuring and restructuring, ironies, special effects—a whole spectrum of privileged communication between Kesey and himself. There is a minimum of editorial explanation (which appears in the typeface of this introduction), and the only changes incorporated have been to make the spelling regular. Punctuation remains the way it was in the heat of composition. Italics are used to indicate Kesey's underlining. These underlinings appear to have been made upon re-reading and indicate importance, highlighting, for further use, note this, etc. Most of the underlinings were made in red and blue.

All the material except the new novel (and, of course the introductions by Malcolm Cowley and J. C. Pratt) is from the University of Oregon archives. There are five large cardboard boxes of materials and a box of tapes in the collection. And since printed space is limited, sections like the working notes leading to **Sometimes A Great Notion** were selected to give the reader something of the feel of going through the boxes and encountering the great variety of material which eventually came together in the novel. We selected to document **SGN** rather than **Cuckoo's Nest** in great detail because the material for **SGN** was more complete and many-faceted and demonstrated the creative process clearly.

The problem of dating the material was so difficult and speculative that no dates appear. Kesey could only put certain materials within a spread of three or four years. Scholars interested in exact dates could do the same from the contents. More importantly, there is a timeless sense of a writer's imagination probing the world around him, fitting disparate parts together, making the act of imagination as vital as Chief Broom's flight across the lawn, Hank Stamper's dogged insistence on the value of one man, and Grandma Whittier's indomitable curiosity and good sense.

ms

Thanks to Martin Schmitt, curator of the University of Oregon Library Special Collections, for his cooperation. We would also like to express our deep appreciation to our patrons and donors (listed at the back of this book), as well as the Coordinating Council of Literary Magazines and the Oregon Arts Commission. And finally, a special thanks to Ken Kesey for his assistance and his permission to use the material of this book. His first published fiction appeared in Volume I, No. 2, Fall 1957, of the **Northwest Review,** a short story, "The First Sunday in September."

# CONTENTS

**EDITOR'S NOTE**      v

**INTRODUCTIONS**

    MALCOLM COWLEY
    Ken Kesey at Stanford      1

    JOHN CLARK PRATT
    On Editing Kesey: Confessions of a Straight Man      5

*ONE FLEW OVER THE CUCKOO'S NEST*
    **(manuscript notes)**      17

*SOMETIMES A GREAT NOTION*      24
    "First Inkling"      25
    "Spring Rain" I      28
    "Spring Rain" II      31
    "Spring Rain" III      34
    Notes on a Night in Florence      42
    The Arrangement      45
    "I haven't settled into a method on this book yet . . ."      50
    "Sometimes I live in the country"
        (manuscript notes)      53
    "Night—a candle, a joint, . ."      57
    "Lee. . ."      58
    "Hank. . ."      60
    Viv/ Hank/ Lee      61
    Lee's hang-up    (manuscript notes)      69
    General notes      70
    "He has been defeated"    (manuscript notes)      73
    The story/ The River, etc.      75
    Manuscript pages      86

**AFTER TWO SUCCESSFUL NOVELS**
  (holograph)                                      95


*SEVEN PRAYERS by Grandma Whittier*
  (part of a new novel)                            99


**ZANE AND JED**                                   169


**"WHY PLANT CORN?"**                              173


**A SCENE FROM THE NOVEL, *ZOO***                  177


**POEMS, ETC.**                                    190

The cover drawing and all other art are by Ken Kesey.
Photos, except as otherwise credited, are from Ken Kesey.

Malcolm Cowley

# KEN KESEY AT STANFORD

Ken Kesey was in my writing class at Stanford in the fall term of 1960. He wasn't there technically, in the sense that I passed in his grade to the administration, but he was there in person and by virtue of what he was writing, which was a novel, then untitled, about the psychiatric ward of a veterans' hospital. Kesey had spent the academic year 1958-59 as a graduate student at Stanford with a creative-writing fellowship. As a matter of courtesy, fellows were invited to attend the class in later years without being formally enrolled. Kesey and Tillie Olsen were two of the earlier fellows whom this instructor was always glad to see.

It was a pretty brilliant class that year, including as it did some professional writers already launched on their careers. Larry McMurtry, for instance, was working on what I think was his second novel, *Leaving Cheyenne*. He was a light, sallow, bespectacled cowboy who wore Texas boots and spoke in a pinched variety of the West Texas drawl. Gradually I learned that he had read almost everything in English literature, besides a great deal in French, and that he had written a dissertation on the scabrous poetry of John Wilmot, Earl of Rochester. Larry supplemented his Stanford fellowship by finding rare books on the ten-cent tables of Salvation Army outlets and reselling them to dealers; *Book Prices Current* was his bible.

Peter S. Beagle was only twenty-one, with plump cheeks and a solemn boyish smile, but the Viking Press had already published his successful first novel, *A Fine and Private Place*. I took a special interest in Peter, since I was a literary adviser for Viking and since I knew and liked his two famous uncles, the painters Raphael and Moses Soyer, but I wasn't able to help him with his new project. He was trying to write an autobiographical novel about his year in Paris, and he was too young for autobiography; his bent was for gentle fantasy and humor. There were other gifted students in the class. I remember James Baker Hall, Judith Rascoe, Arvin Brown (now with the Yale School of the Drama),

1

Gurney Norman, and Joanna Ostrow, who was the most beautiful woman I encountered in twenty years of teaching. It is hard to understand how Frank O'Connor, who succeeded me in the winter quarter, could bear to drop her from the class. Joanna had talent as well as beauty, but I suppose that she didn't manifest enough literary devotion to satisfy O'Connor's tough standards.

The class of fifteen assembled in the Jones Room at a huge oval table. One student would read his work aloud and others would offer comments. My problem at the head of the table was how to get the class working together. I believed that young writers learn more from one another than they do from an older instructor. I knew that their comments on stories revealed two contradictory impulses: first, to assert their egos by putting down their rivals; second, to advance the cause of good writing in an unselfish fashion by making useful suggestions. Aggression and *agape*. My tactic was always to put down the putter-downers and always to encourage the suggestions. In a good class like the one at Stanford in 1960, *agape* won out, jealousies were submerged, and stories were sometimes vastly improved in their second and third drafts.

I don't remember any comments that Kesey made. I do remember that he looked stolid and self-assured as he sat near the other end of the table. He had the build of a plunging halfback, with big shoulders and a neck like the stump of a Douglas fir. Chapters of his novel were read aloud in class and they aroused a mixed but generally admiring response. The instructor was excited by having found something original. Later Kesey showed me the whole of the unfinished manuscript and we discussed it in private sessions. Did I contribute anything? "Not even a sentence" is the answer; the book is Kesey's from the first word to the last. Probably I pointed out passages that didn't "work," that failed to produce a desired effect on the reader. Certainly I asked questions, and some of these may have helped to clarify Kesey's notions of how to go about solving his narrative problems, but the solutions were always his own.

From the beginning he had his narrator in the person of Chief Broom, a schizophrenic Indian who pretends to be deaf and dumb. He had his own crazy visions—induced by eating peyote, as he later explained—and these could be attributed to Chief Broom. Thus, when the Indian looks at Big Nurse, "She's swelling up, swells till her back's splitting out the white uniform and she's let her arms section out long enough to wrap around the three of them five, six times . . . she blows up bigger and bigger, big as a tractor, so big I can smell the machinery inside the way you smell a motor pulling too big a load." That hallucinated but everyday style, smelling of motor oil, was something new in fiction. Kesey's narrative problem, the central one, was how to use Chief Broom-or-Bromden's visions as the medium for telling an essentially simple, dramatic, soundly constructed story.

His first drafts must have been written at top speed; they were full of typing errors, as if the words had come piling out of a Greyhound bus too fast to have their clothes brushed. Later Kesey would redo the manuscript and correct most of the misspellings. He had his visions, but he didn't have the fatal notion of some Beat writers, that the first hasty account of a vision was a sacred text not to be tampered with. He revised, he made deletions and additions; he was working with readers in mind. I continued to be excited by Kesey's work as the manuscript grew longer (though I couldn't share his faith in the Randle P. McMurphy system of psychotherapy). I remember sending enthusiastic reports to Viking. A year later I was delighted when the manuscript arrived in the Viking office, this time with a title: *One Flew Over the Cuckoo's Nest.*

After turning over the advanced writing course to O'Connor—in private life Michael O'Donovan—I had spent the winter quarter at Stanford with less challenging assignments. Michael was a dear man with an Irish temper who wouldn't stand for nonsense. He couldn't have felt much sympathy for Kesey's narrator or his style or his hero. I heard that Kesey had stopped attending classes in the Jones Room and was persuading others to stay away too, sometimes by inviting them to his house on Perry Lane and keeping them there with drinks and conversation until the class was over. He had become the man whom other young rebels tried to imitate, almost like Hemingway in Montparnasse during the 1920s.

I paid perhaps two visits to Perry Lane, which was the Left Bank of Stanford, but the visit I remember was on the night when Kesey and his wife were throwing a big party. Most of the advanced writing class was there, with other friends of the Keseys including Vic Lovell, a graduate student with bold notions about psychology and a ducktail haircut. On a table by the window was a huge bowl of green punch from which clouds of mist or steam

3

kept rising. Kesey explained that the punch was brewed with Kool-Aid and dry ice; the mist was carbon dioxide. "It looks like the sort of punch that Satan would serve," I said while politely accepting half a cupful. Was it the famous punch that Kesey had spiked with LSD? I haven't the faintest notion because I never drained my cup. Instead I wandered out to the kitchen, where my wife was talking with Faye Kesey and admiring the baby. I fell into conversation with Ken's Grandmother. "If you don't like punch," she said, "I brought along a bottle of bootleg whiskey from Arkansas." "That suits me just fine," I said, taking a pull at the bottle. By that time the crowd around the punch bowl was growing noisy. Arvin Brown, who drank several cupfuls of the green stuff, tells me that he didn't recover full consciousness for twenty-four hours.

John Clark Pratt

# ON EDITING KESEY:
## CONFESSIONS OF A STRAIGHT MAN

Whoever Ken Kesey may really be, he's still writing and is alive and well in Oregon. That is my first and last real "confession," not because there is too little to say but because there is really too much—and to attempt an actual confessional might well imply that I believe in the kind of order which Kesey himself neither possesses nor admits. True, Ken does throw the Ching—and records each instance in his Ching Book with its beautifully ornate cover—but because order for Kesey somehow results from a combination of chance and individual perception, what I offer here are some personal comments about how I and a few other "straights" have perceived during the past few years the phenomenon which is Ken Kesey, his writing and his clan.

First of all, I don't claim to have edited Kesey, either. What I did was convince the Viking Press that a Critical Edition of *One Flew Over the Cuckoo's Nest* was a good idea. Then I put it together. The result was what Kesey, trying to explain to his son Jed who I was and what I was doing in Oregon, called "that blue copy" of his novel. When the edition came out in 1973, Kesey told me that he liked it and had placed it on an honored shelf—beside the throne. Traditional not only in this sense, the Keseys keep books in their bathroom.

During my most recent visit to the farm last May, I looked for the blue copy, but like so many other books Kesey says he has "right over there," it was missing. "Someone must be reading it," Kesey growled. The bathroom, however, was the same. The two-foot wide, three-foot deep inverted aluminum cone still serves as a sink (though no longer, I suspect, as a baby's bath), and the side door of the bathroom still opens toward the blacktop road.

There never has been a real front door to the Keseys' house; and the original driveway which used to lead up to the bathroom door has been blocked off. "They all just kept dropping in," Faye says. Now one enters through a side door into a long hall lined with hats, coats, jackets, boots, notes on the wall, jars, cans, and tools—directly into the kitchen, where it seems that Faye is always cooking something for someone if she's not acting as Ken's business manager and correspondence secretary, taking a group of children on a camping trip, or ministering in her mild, effective way to the assortment of family, friends, associates, lawyers, editors, and just plain hangers-on who flow in and out of the Kesey's place.

I first saw the barn in December of 1971. "Look for the star," Faye had told me on the phone. "You can't miss it. We live in a red barn with a star on it." Resembling a World War II Army Air Corps insignia, the large, painted star does dominate the side of the barn, and the bus now squats a few hundred feet away. In 1971, though, I could not see the bus from the road—*the* bus —the Kesey-Babbs-Cassady cross-country bus which was then parked around back. Half covered with rolling folds of plastic, the day-glo painted swirls on its hood and sides barely visible, the bus when I first saw it looked like a giant cocoon. It was in the bus, said Martin Schmitt of the University of Oregon Library, that he found manuscript material for *Cuckoo's Nest* beneath one of the seats. The pages were dirty and being leaked on from one of the windows. Even in 1971, the bus had not run for years; and it does not run now. It has been moved to a pasture where it serves as a dugout for the kids' baseball team. "We towed it with a tractor," Ken said. There are no plans to move it again. Even Babbs' bus, a smaller version of *the* bus, has been sold—so now only the star and the rather distinct dugout differentiate the Kesey farm from all the others like it in the valley.

Just before Christmas five years ago I found Kesey's star in a heavy Oregon rain. Inside, a live, ornamented holly tree commanded a corner of the living area. Beside it, on a perch half as high as the seven-foot tree, was the parrot who still squawks "Hi," "Bye," and occasionally, "Ken." Two large white cats raced up and down the branches of the tree, causing the spiked leaves to rustle and shed ornaments. Occasionally there would also be a child in the tree—catching cats. Also rustling and flapping from the wind was the entire far wall of the dining area, an expanse of plastic tacked to wall studs where the glass would someday go. The exposed barn beams were hung with clothes, tack, and implements, and behind the large zodiac brightly painted on the floor, the stairs which go nowhere led up to a second story which does not exist. That winter, it may have been Hagen, I think, who told me his idea for raising and controlling Oregon's water table. His scheme involved the construction of a giant water glass, many miles in circumference, which would when inverted control the water level on the acreage it enclosed. There were some mechanical problems, he admitted, but the principle worked in the laboratory. While he was talking, Paul Foster's wife nursed their daughter Euphoria, then just a few weeks old.

The entire clan was assembling, too, from town and from other farms. "We're going to de-ball the calves," Kesey announced shortly after my arrival. "Everybody's coming." Meanwhile, Faye was getting the children ready for the Christmas play; someone was playing something by the Grateful Dead in another part of the barn (I found out later it was the office, in a loft over the garage); the lights were flickering and failing because of an erratic power source; Ken Babbs, tall, thin, intense, was telling me how it really was to fly helicopters in the early days of Vietnam; and I, ostensibly the straightest of the straight, short hair and all, having taught in uniform the day before as a faculty member of the Air Force Academy, a year back from a Southeast Asia combat tour but armed this time only with admiration for Kesey and a great love for *Cuckoo's Nest,* was there to meet the people, ask some questions, gather some material, and hopefully to do something productive for my edition of Kesey's novel.

Within an hour, I was rolling in a muddy pasture trying to affix rubber bands to the testicles of calves. "We don't cut them off," Kesey said. "This way doesn't hurt as much. After a little while, they just fall off." There were at least fifteen of us: some chased calves while others bulldogged; and taking turns working the cameras, sound, and lights, people were always filming. "It's for 'The Movie'," Ken explained during a breather. My feet hurt. One of the boots Kesey had loaned me was too small; the other was too large. As I threw myself at a galloping calf which was larger than the rest, Kesey yelled, "Let that one go. He's got too much spirit to be a steer." I suggested that we name him Bromden. "Yeah," Kesey said. "The Chief."

We cleaned up for the play, the traditional nativity story to be performed at the Pleasant Hill school. One of the Kesey children was in it, and as we entered the gymnasium, the rain on the roof sounded like marbles. We climbed into the bleachers, Faye and I and Ken and Paul Foster, his little red eyes gleaming through a mass of black curls, and Paul's wife carrying Euphoria who disturbed the scene first by crying, then by slurping as she nursed. A few heads kept turning our way. Once, when a young, costumed wise man on the stage forgot what came after "gold" and "fff--rr--ankincense," Kesey growled loudly: "And a canned ham." Leaning forward, elbows on knees, Kesey was recognizable only by the top of his head. The tight cap with the curls of reddish hair sticking out around it resembled a busted softball. When the play was over, Ken applauded enthusiastically, then joined the carol singing, loudly and off key. Then we went back to the barn and stayed up all night, talking.

That was my introduction to "editing" Kesey. I did get a look at the *Garage Sale* galleys, in which the ward drawings done by Kesey are torturedly beautiful. I also did a sketch of the barn's interior and wrote pages in my journal, both of which have been misplaced. I asked Ken all the standard and irrelevant questions about the creation of his novel ("How long did it take you?" "Oh, I don't know.") I slept in the little house with the cats beside the tiny pond in which Ken claims there are six-pound bass and watched, in the fine mist of morning, *something* surge and heave beneath the water across the pond near the sagging and overgrown fishing boat. And I slipped and fell, as Faye had warned me not to, on the slick wooden ramp which led down to the cabin after the long night which culminated with Ken's throwing the Ching for me and predicting bright things.

It's been a similar scene since. Once, even though my visit had been arranged for a long time, I arrived to a note from Faye saying that Ken was in Los Angeles, that she would be in the mountains for the night, that Babbs was on his way over, and that I should make myself at home. That time, I helped Babbs pile rocks on his new bridge, trout fished with two of his many children, talked again late into the night about the war, the state of the world, how our children were going astray (Babbs' son wanted to be a professional football player), and traded tunes on a guitar, the amplifiers set up beside the river. Between swats at mosquitoes, Babbs played "Blue Moon" and "Five Foot Two," not, as I first thought, merely in honor of my apparent straightness but because he had learned to play the ukelele in college and has not, he still claims, progressed much further.

I note these incidents because they often do not reflect the Kesey and Babbs portrayed in *The Electric Kool-Aid Acid Test*, the main source of the Kesey mystique. It is a book which Kesey has called "ninety-six per-cent accurate," but it does not reflect the current scene on the farm. Anomalies abound, and as a straight man in most senses of the word, I have perceived a definite under-current of seriousness and, yes, straightness, not only in Kesey's writings but in his actions as well. There is still, of course, the expected zaniness. In May, for instance, Kesey and Babbs con-ducted an impromptu briefing (this time for my benefit) using the farm's aerial photographs which are tacked to the wall beside the round dining table. "Now," Kesey said, pointing at a road intersection with a pencil, "Ve send ze tanks down zis back road, here." "Ja, Mein Herr," answered Babbs, "Und zon ve bring in ze fighter-bombers mit napalm to get ze command post." As they bantered for fully ten minutes, I noted how much military jargon Babbs had retained from his Marine Corps experience. "You should hear him a week before you get here," Kesey said. "He sounds like a general." The "briefing" concluded, we took a drive in one of Kesey's aging convertibles ("I'm trying to corner the market," he says) to get gas for his tractor.

To me, this zaniness seems somehow residual—and I realize that this comment may not sit well with either the members or the worshippers of Kesey's clan—but I believe that the essential seriousness which compels most people who really care about anything is beginning to surface at the Keseys. It is not enough, I think, merely to note that all of them are thirteen years older than they were when they careened across the country blowing not only their minds but everyone else's as well; but maturity is certainly a factor in the change. Additionally, however, one should note that only once has Kesey really written about the way he has lived—in the viewplay in *Garage Sale* entitled "Over the Bor-der." This script though, is really a group effort written by nobody in particular. *Cuckoo's Nest* (the novel, *not* the movie), *Some-times A Great Notion*, many of the serious essays in *Garage Sale*, the concept and much of the content of the new magazine, *Spit in the Ocean*, and the fragments I have seen of Kesey's new novel are all finely wrought and extremely—well—serious. That Kesey has actually run for a School Board post, has organized and con-ducted the pioneering Media Referendum on political issues, and will constantly remind you that he is, after all, a serious artist—

all of this belies the decade-old impression which many still have of him. Nevertheless, there are still a dwindling number of college dropouts who appear at the farm from time to time, seeking nirvana and the word, but they find as I have something different, something that's not quite what the myth says it should be.

That a worldwide cult of Keseyphiles exists is obvious, but I suspect that when his new novel is published, readers who appreciate Kesey only for *Cuckoo's Nest* will be at least startled if not openly distressed. Creating a novel, Kesey believes, is strictly an individual effort, and when writing fiction, he keeps very much to himself, often working for long periods, sleeping, then going back to work immediately. Faye rarely sees him during these periods, she says; nor does anyone else. Perhaps the innate seriousness of the real Kesey may exist only in his fiction—the individual author with an individual artistic vision. As with *Over the Border*, much of the post-1964 material bearing Kesey's name has been created by the group, but I think that Kesey at heart is not a group person. He attracts people around him, but he is not himself a joiner.

He is, however, one of the best role players I have ever seen, and he is almost impossible to pin down (I suspect this phrase would apply to his well-known wrestling skills, too). As I have mentioned elsewhere, he still refuses to admit that he knew of Billy Budd's stuttering when he modeled his Billy Bibbit upon Melville's character, and his fiction abounds with enough deadly serious tweaks at literary tradition that his allusions have given some "straight" critics fits. While not strictly the concern of this essay, Kesey's multi-valent fictional technique should never be ignored.

Practically everyone has had trouble with Kesey in one way or another. I have yet, for instance, to find in print a coherent commentary written by a medical person about *Cuckoo's Nest*. There have been some nervous disclaimers voiced by disgruntled psychiatrists since the movie appeared, but in general, the profession has been silent. The novel is quite often used in psychology as well as literature courses, and one would expect more published criticism. I do know that the doctors have been reading the book. Too late for the Critical Edition, I received a letter from a British psychiatrist who was practicing in Canada. His "initial impressions" follow:

i. The description of the narrator suggests a drug-induced psychosis, not schizophrenia as is implied.

ii. The main critical element of the book is aimed at an individual and her misuse and distortion of psychiatric treatment methods rather than at these methods themselves. (Equivalent to Soviet distortions of communist theory or some American distortion of democracy of recent vintage?)

iii. There is excessively dramatic presentation of some elements, ECT [Electro Convulsive Therapy] being one. Standard current [sic] practice now is a very 'low-key' procedure modified with short acting barbituates and muscle relaxants . . . . No explanation of its action is adequate as yet; however, it does *not* act by suppressing memory or some non-specific "mass action" brain damage effect (i.e. blunt instrument theory).

(Have you read Julian Huxley's autobiography? His description and attitudes re his own treatment with ECT may help balance it a bit better.)

iv. There is the inevitable Freudian theme and in this, as in other ways, he appears to subscribe to that which he appears to be criticising.

v. The diagnostic label placed on the central character would appear to be wrong—i.e. he is not describing a "psychopath." He more or less says this anyway.

vi. The study you didn't believe existed was Caudhill, 1949 (Yale). (The TV incident would appear to be a steal from this report.) Several other such studies "from the inside" have been made. Details if you want them.

vii. Overall impression. If that sort of thing exists it is barbaric. Suggests:

1. Compartments with separate hierarchies, e.g. nursing not open to medical or patient criticism.

2. Incompetent medical staff unable to properly use any treatment mode . . . .

Many of the above professional insights are relevant and intriguing; all that is really missing is a sense of the metaphoric nature of art. There is a final note, however, which is alarming. The psychiatrist concludes,

Since reading the book I have found that the supervisor of nursing gave it to all the nurses on our 25-bed unit to read and then issued a series of edicts ending ". . . we must show them (the patients) that we are in control"—*using the book as justification!*

Ah McMurphy! Ah humanity!

In contrast to the lack of response from the medical profession, Kesey certainly has provoked feminists. From his personal reputation and his traditionally dominant central male characters, Kesey has generated much resentment from women who decry both the swaggering McMurphy (whom they see as Kesey himself) and the sniveling, female-dominated Bibbit. Marcia Falk's letter in the Critical Edition which castigates Walter Kerr as well as Kesey is a strident example, and as "editor" I found myself unenviably caught between Ms. Falk and *The New York Times*. Her original letter having been gelded by the *Times*, Ms. Falk requested that I print a restored version. The permissions editor of the *Times* would have none of this; she emphasized the long-standing policy of her paper that no changes be made in a reprint. Neither could I use brackets which would disturb the purity of the text. No less directly polite, Ms. Falk pressed for her original wording. The result, agreed upon by both women, was a Keseyian compromise—a footnote at the end of the *Times* letter, a parenthetical entry which speaks, I think, for itself. Whether in terms of "balls" or "sexual parts," Kesey provokes.

Not all women agree, however. I know some young Portuguese, a group of University students, who as late as 1975 had never heard of Kesey—or for that matter of Joseph Heller, Thomas Pynchon, or Kurt Vonnegut. Having just experienced what to them was a major political awakening, they were eager to read anything new from the United States. My female students became especially fascinated with *Cuckoo's Nest*. Most of them from quite wealthy families, the girls were usually very well dressed, impeccably groomed and made up, poised, polite, and by any standards, beautiful. We discussed the role of the Big Nurse, the male-female opposition as symbol, and the general belief by Europeans that American men in fact have become Bibbitts or Hardings. It was different, they told me, in Portugal. Portuguese men were always in control; they ran things; they dominated. But what if, I asked, what if the new Portugal with its democratization and its equality were to see the traditional male role decline?—perhaps to become (horrors) similar to that of *Cuckoo's Nest*? It could never happen, the women all agreed. The Big Nurse could never survive in Portugal. Why not? "It is quite simple," one dark haired girl said, sitting very straight and looking imperiously at me. "It couldn't happen here, because we—the women—won't permit it." Like so many other reactions to what Kesey writes, there are no ambiguities here.

So far I have been commenting upon the public Kesey—the man who appears to others in person or through his works. Let me conclude by mentioning another aspect of my "editing" experience, one which only a very small number of people can experience. As readers of this special Kesey issue now know, the Kesey collection in the University of Oregon library, while not mammoth (there is much more material in the Prankster Archives) is nevertheless extensive. The collection consists of letters, manuscripts, working notes and tapes. A product of Martin Schmitt's perseverance and Kesey's sense of the need to preserve, these papers are now practically inaccessible—in part because of what I have been told was the habit of previous users to take souvenirs home. Thanks to a handwritten note from Faye, I was an early viewer of the collection, and I wish I could have included more of the Kesey-Babbs correspondence in the blue book. Kesey's letters are intensely personal and very, very Victorian in their length and inclusiveness. They abound with literary comments, descriptions of events and characters of the Prankster years, and impressions of the general American scene. The tapes are equally rich, but because there are so many I doubt if anyone has listened to all of them.

The manuscripts, however, provide an "editor" with a different experience. Many of them are early, hence usually bad fiction, but relatively intact are the working notes and the drafts for *Cuckoo's Nest*. It is always a thrill for a scholar to use original manuscripts—to be able to see how characters evolve from draft to draft—to note major and minor structural changes as the novel grows—to perhaps be able to *feel*, even as the author may have, when an emendation clicks and a scene works. In previous research, I had watched, one hundred years afterward, as George Eliot shaped *Middlemarch*, and I had a similar experience with the manuscripts of *Cuckoo's Nest*.

One page, filed in a miscellaneous folder, stays with me. That Kesey, often high on drugs, wrote some of the passages during his night duties as a ward attendant is widely believed and probably true, but the holograph page entitled "Names" does much more for an "editor" than merely corroborate a fable. The subtitle identifies the drug, the handwriting varies in size, slant, and legibility, the comments are impressionistic and fragmentary, and many of the words are lined out or doodled over. Kesey claims not to remember exactly when this page was written—but it is a very early set of notes. Beneath the title, Kesey's scrawl offers the following: [see holograph reproduction pages 17-23]

lsd impressions

Sanchez — Samuels?        Broom  Birehnski
Harding — Harling

Wr , fi [lined through]
    Wire, fire, lumber <lock> [lined through]
    I thought of how the cuckoo's nest was
so big, so big, to hold all the birds in it.
Not like a nest so much as like a - - -
       ?
    ONe Flew OVer the Cuckoo's nest [superimposed
              over the question mark, above]
See that big goose up there against
the moon — alone — wings spread
in a black cross.
    This means McMurphy is a wild goose
Dwell on the beauty of wild geese, the
magisty. Get some good visions of


    Canadian Honkers booming        [verso]
    down the Columbia Gorge
Bivishki [lined through]    Birenshki
    Nurse with a fingertip painted red-hot
    as a soldering iron.  Handful of fire.
    Handful of lighted cigarettes — when she
    lays that hand on you its so awful hot or
    so awful cold you can't tell which.
    I'm writing across smiles, grimaces, eyes,
    winks, flashes of light, noses, teeth ——

14

> Nurse with her lips and fingernails that funny
> off color — reflecting each other — flight of
> metaphors — heat, cold, fire, madison avenue, orange,
> complexion like a popsical, — enamel complexion.
> The rest of the point went well, but they
> blew it when they got to the lips + fingertips.

Nurse Birenshki had not yet become Nurse Ratched, but her character, as well as the basic metaphor for McMurphy and also the title for the novel can be seen emerging on the page. Kesey's literary ambiguities came later with revision; what we can see here is the moment of conception of a work of art.

To resolve many of Kesey's personal and artistic ambiguities is impossible, especially for the majority of people who know only *Cuckoo's Nest* (the book, *not* the movie. I have already had the sad duty of reminding a student that the *book* does not have an elaborate basketball scene and that Candy gets rather bruised in the novel but not on the screen. His paper failed.) Still as popular in classrooms as it was during the late 60's, the novel is attracting a younger readership than before. Many high schools require it now, but few of the students know anything at all about its author, and very few indeed read *Kool-Aid Acid Test* either before or after *Cuckoo's Nest*. Many of the younger readers are truly frightened by what they think the novel says, unlike the previous generation (yes, Ken, generation) of readers who only a few years ago saw in McMurphy's rebellion and Bromden's "escape" a symbol of their own psychological, social ,and political plight. What these younger students do know about Kesey is a mixture of fable and fantasy which produces statements such as "Oh, yeah, he's the one who wrote the movie," or "It's too bad his mind got shot from all those hard drugs." Neither belief, I'm pleased to confess, is true.

What *is* true about Ken Kesey is that he is working hard on the magazine and writing a novel from the point of view of an aged woman, Ma Whittier.* The plastic windbreak in the dining room has finally been replaced by a sliding glass door through which one can still see an occasional swirl on the surface of the small pond. Paul Foster, whose intricate drawings so dominate *Garage Sale,* has left the fold and is now seriously preaching the Christian gospel. The zodiac on the living room floor is often covered by a wrestling mat. The office now occupies a separate building. Ken Babbs' bridge is complete and has withstood one major flood, and his "ranch" consists of the bridge, four pigs, two cows, and a roughed out foundation which will contain a house, he hopes, someday. There is talk of college among the children, and it's obvious that the frantic obsession with motion which so characterized the Pranksters of the mid-sixties has given way to a distinct and rather conventionally straight sense of place. Looking around his acreage beside one of the loveliest rivers I have ever seen, Babbs said, "You know, it's the best place in the world to be poor in," and he doubts with Kesey that the bus will ever roll again. What is accelerating, however, is the reputation of the magazine and the number of Ma Whittier's memoirs—and I suspect that before too long there will be a definite answer to *Rolling Stone's* plaintive cry, "Write us another novel, Ken." As a matter of fact, I'll bet on it.

* See the selection on p. 99.

John Clark Pratt edited the Viking Critical Edition of Kesey's *One Flew Over the Cuckoo's Nest*. A Vietnam veteran, he taught at the United States Air Force Academy for 14 years before becoming chairman of the English Department, Colorado State University. His publications include *The Laotian Fragments* (1974), which he describes as "an unsung novel about the Vietnam war."

Names

Cut impresions

Sawlog — ~~Samuels~~ Bromm Bivekoski

Harding — Harling

~~the life~~

~~Wind, fire, water look~~

I thought of how the cuchoo's nest was
so big, so big, to hold all the birds in it.
Not like a nest so much as like a - - -


ONe FLew OVer the Cuckoo's nest

See that big goose up there against
the moon — alone — wings spread
in a black cross.

This means Mc Murphy is a wild goose
Dwell on the beauty of wild geese, the
majesty. Get some good visions of

17

Canadian Honkers booming
down the Columbia Gorge


~~Brishki~~ Birenski

Nurse with a fingertip pointed red – hot
as a soldering iron. Handful of fire.
Handful of lighted cigarettes – when she
lays that hand on you its so awful hot or
so awful cold you can't tell which.
   I'm writing across smiles, grimaces, eyes,
inks flashes of light, noses, ~~teeth~~

Nurse with her lips and fingernails that funny
off color – reflecting each other – flight of
metaphors – hot, cold, fire, madison avenue orange,
complexion like a popsical, – enamel complexion.
The rest of the point went well, but they
blew it when they got to the lips or fingertips.

18

face face face face her face, his face
its face, eyes, teeth, & wrinkles, hair,
face, face face, face

Say it till the word is strange in your
head — fay — ssss fay hiss — off-ace


something on every page to do with
a face — (look, feel of face, touch of
face, half of face, chunk of face

Faces pouring over Biwinski

Biwinski — I am Biwinski — Biwinski
is Sanchez — Sanchez is Biwinski — I am
Biwinski — Biwinski's face is mine.
Sanchez Face Biwinski Sanchez Face Me
Biwinski Sanchez Face Me Mine Me Biwinski

19

Those eyes, faces, — Mc Murphy tore
them out to in front to my the eyes
and takes them on him.

gradually — as and Mc Murphy steps
on the ward — the eyes turn from
Bimvinsky to Mc murphy.

brown and hard as a turkseye eye

confetti of face

glass of face,

machine of face

broken rainbows — broken
covenant.

her book clatters against your dry, busty, stand of a twig caught in a paper sack.

looked out and saw a sky clean and blue as iron.

hear the womp of somebody shaking tin clothes like fishnets

faces flowing like a million shredded sunday funnies — eyes, noses, cheeks, profiles — a confetti of face

suits like eyes looking at you from the side of their lips.

There's an $ eye on my knuckle – my whole hand is a face, working to tell me

the chrome gleam of a flashlight in a black hand, *like a drone* waiting to strike out with its light.

A flower like a fourth of july burst frozen and its long arching green fire stalk put down in a face

② Sometimes I got to feel this wall to believe it – flat, blat, cold – but when I put a cheekbone up against it (pappy, how can you hear a train coming by ~~putting~~ ~~teeth~~ biting the rail in your teeth?) I pick up the machinery they're trying to keep secret from me.

Sounds – wailings, doo doo <u>doos</u>, signals some poor guy upstairs is putting out through the tube in his shoulder

22

Sometimes there's a mechanical bird sit out the window, wound to breaking, and the high ~~scale~~ than screeches he makes cuts me like a mule whips, leaves flesh hang off me in long, ~~white~~ ~~ripped~~ strips.

An airplane flew in one window and out the other, after circling the room a couple of ~~times~~.

"We want to love you ~~understand yourselves~~

There's a scuffle down the hall — old man shedding ~~clothes~~ layers of tinfoil.

His eyes inching over his grin, like headlights over a big truck grill — shiny, hard, petroleum gloss.

23

This section is a collection of material leading to **Sometimes A Great Notion:** "First Inkling of SGN," the "Spring Rain" story idea, working notes, diagrams, character and story development notes, manuscript pages. The sections are continuous except as indicated by three asterisks.

Try to make Hank give up.

Hank: "If we don't get him this round we'll get him the next."

The following three pages were marked, "First Inkling of SGN." The last page is the back of the previous page and records additions numbered one and two.

Most of the men who take their lives up into the ~~Oregon Coast woods~~ logging ~~~~ camps ~~~~ ~~after the big monthly check~~

Most of the men who take their lives up into the Northern logging camps come to be content with leaving a piece of ~~the value~~ behind every season -- a finger ~~but guess~~ lopped off last year, six square inches of thigh hide this season, maybe an eye next year -- as if it ~~is~~ only fair ~~to them~~ to leave the ~~land~~ something in ~~trade~~ return for the the timber they ~~tore~~ away. After five or ten seasons of such trading the men ~~begin to feel~~ they've been drifted along the line someplace and ~~you just gotta~~ play it a little closer to the belt, ~~settle for less~~ money lower stakes, mill jobs and paper work, less to gain, sure, but who's about to ~~risk getting stuck?~~ play a steady winner?

~~In the Wacanda woods area~~
~~a~~ One stocking little logger, called Bunt by his buddies, had beat ~~the~~ ~~succeeded in history of~~ woods. In sixteen years ~~of logging~~ he had ~~never~~ got more than ~~bruised~~ ~~~~. He ~~was~~ always seemed ~~to hop out~~ out of the way before an accident started. If the wind was about to blow a limb off overhead he quickened his choppy little step enough to always someplace else. The men said of him, "If you can keep up with Bunt nothing's gonna drop on you. The trees can't touch

him. It's like ~~try~~ tryna drop a log on a ~~running mouse.~~ lucky mouse."

"It aint luck," Blunt said. "There aint no luck in the woods. It's the _feel_!" He made an odd, pawing motion at the green tangle of sloshing and fern, like a bear raking food to his mouth. "The feel, you know? You got to You just ~~go along~~ loose and fast, is ~~much.~~ what. You got it or you don't."

Whatever it was, ~~he had enough~~ it was adequate enough to keep him alive and unbroken in the woods ~~bots going out though he hadn't~~ ~~planned it~~ ~~that money to years~~ the money saved ~~in that it years required for him~~ a small sawmill of his own, ~~its~~ foundation for a house on a choice ~~right~~ shoreside right on the Wacanda Auga, and a bawillы. He hadnt planned it this way. ~~in case~~ The money that went into the bank was just ~~that~~. He hadnt planned. From the ~~day~~ the real estate ~~quot~~ drew the loggers attention to the money he had amassed in the bank and convinced him he was wealthy enough to be a business man and not just a logger, clinching the sale of the mill by throwing in the house right and foundation from ~~them~~ on ~~his~~ life that had been like air for him to see into become increasingly cluttered and ~~monday~~

The real estate ~~now~~ wasn't unloading a white elephant and meant only good for the logger, but from the day of the sale Blunts life, which had been clear to him as the air he breathed, became increasingly cluttered and monkey.

① and ~~make him a good wage~~ enough
money in ~~seven teen~~ that after seventeen
~~years he had~~

and build a bank account large
enough to afford him

② ~~left~~ ~~in to pocket~~ the
amount of the previous month's pay that
~~remained when~~ he still had left when he got
payed again. He deposited it to make room
for the next check, ~~never keeping~~ track of
~~the growing account~~ and might never have
had any idea of the amount in his name if
a ~~small~~ ~~little~~ loud man hadn't heard of it
~~this from the bank teller~~. He made it his business
to see that Bennt put his money to work
for him. He went to see the logger in the hotel room
above the restaurant, He carried a shoebox of papers
and ~~he~~ charts and pictures with him. After
less than an hour he had convinced the logger
that a man with a ~~such a sum to~~
his name was by right a business man, ~~and not~~ not
a log ~~bum~~, He sold him a fine little log mill a few
miles from Wacgala, at a fair price with reasonable payments,
~~and even~~ even throw in the house foundation and
property to boot because they belonged to the mill ~~to~~ owner (over)

27

Here is a succession of drafts of a single story, "Spring Rain," which eventually became SOMETIMES A GREAT NOTION. The stories are arranged as drafts of a developing idea, a process of names, impressions, actions and settings. Joe Ben and Hank Stamper, the Oregon woods and rain, these, even in the third version of the story, only hint at the final richness in SGN. But in these three manuscripts a fragment may be seen in the process of becoming. These are drafts and never meant for publication in this form. The only change made for print is that spelling has been made regular.

[I.]     SPRING RAIN

kesey

Suddenly rain is falling. Not from the sky overhead—above through the glittering tips of the firs the boy can see the sky still shining clear and blue—but falling from the south, where the mountains stand like a bright green wall in the sunshine. "It don't seem hardly fair, goddamn it. Not even falling, you come right down to it, but being blowed at you from behind the mountains from clouds you couldn't even *see! It don't hardly seem right, rain like this from a pretty sky like that . . ."*

He sprints through the slashing blackberry and salmonberry vines, his face furious, pulling up the hood of his sweatshirt as he runs. The forest is filled with the sound of drops splitting down through pine needles, like scores of skillets somewhere, frying meat. The sun bobs along beside him, no longer offering warmth, no longer a sun but a shabby fraud constructed of wire and gold foil, flashing foolishly in and out of the dripping underbrush. *It don't seem right that a hawk will kill a pigeon, a woodchuck eat a frog . . . who was that papa had in bed this morning?*

"And there ain't a cloud in the sky," he mutters, running. "Not a mothering cloud." But already he can see the woods around him darkening, and when he reaches the wire fence at the edge of the forest the sun is gone and the last scrap of blue being driven out of sight to the north before the charging rain. *Who was that this morning, I wonder?*

Beyond the fence is the graveled ridge of a railroad embankment; when the boy has climbed to the second wire he finds that, past the embankment in a grassy clearing, he can see an old abandoned logging camp. Along with an array of machinery he sees a number of small buildings, most of them crumbling with decay but one shack still looking dry enough for shelter. Standing on the wire the boy pauses, smiling into the rain, pleased by his discovery. Along with the buildings and the ungainly pieces of machinery that dribble rust into the grass, there ranges a number of smaller objects that look almost as promising—unopened crates, cans, bottles, a hard hat, a boot with its green tongue dripping . . . and in the center of the clearing, moored by dozens of cables that should easily bring a half cent a pound at Stokes', stands the spar tree. "And it the first day of May, too." Like a pole for the clutter to dance about. "Boy oh boy," he says, looking across at the solemn circling of junk, "That's all right, that Maypole dance . . ." *But this morning I get out of bed and it's nice and clear and sunny, till I go in the kitchen. Then I see what went on again. There's beer cans everywhere, and dead cigars, and cigarette butts with lipstick. Sure, with lipstick.* ". . . That's kind of all right, even in the rain." *Pink lipstick. Sweet, pale pink. Poor little pigeon, whoever you are this time, poor little pink frog . . . you just don't know, I guess.*

He drops from the fence and starts toward the tracks, still smiling, but before he can fight his way through the green snarl of berryvines that choke the embankment ditch a sudden screech shoots out of the forest down the tracks followed by the Syverson Company log train that comes down out of the South Fork once every few months with Syverson's lumber, and the look of terrific anger and frustration once more clamps the boy's handsome features. *And it ain't right, goddamn it, that you don't know! That nobody knows! It aint fair that everybody be sucked in by him again and again without no warning!*

He climbs from the vines and stands at the edge of the track, close enough to the train that he can see red drops appearing on the backs of his hands and his coat as the streaming wheels swirl rusty water on him. He stands with his shoulders cupping inwards about his chest and curses the train as it passes. He can see the tarpaper roofs of the dry shacks flash between the cars as they bang past. He curses his luck forlornly, telling himself that he should know better'n to expect better; sixteen years on the Oregon Coast should *condition* a guy against being upset by a sudden spring rain or a cold wind, or a log train cutting him off from shelter. These things shouldn't get to him. Not in *this* country, not *this* time of year . . . *but if you can't trust what's behind sunshine and blue skies, what can you trust? Him with his grin and cigar. And what about her, with her sweet pink lipstick? Maybe behind that make-up she's got a beak like a pair of scissors, else what would she need a paint job for? Maybe you can't trust what's behind nothing but for what's behind your own goddamn hide . . .*

"I'm goin' papa." He threw the stained cigarette butt back to the table with the beer cans. "Papa?" he called toward the bedroom. "You hear me? I'm goin' out. Not to school. It's a nice day an' I think I'll take my bike and ride out and cut me some brush."

There was no sound from the bedroom, but through the jarred door he saw a face rise out of the tumble of blankets and turn into the sunshine that beamed through the hole in his father's windowshade. The face squinted at the boy for a moment, then asked, "No classes today?"

"I need some money," the boy answered. "I aim to ride out before all the other kids start, and locate me some real choice brush."

The face smiled—jovial, disarming, an expression aimed at more than just him, the boy knew—and fell back to the blankets. "Fine with me," the boy heard his father call. Then, after a muffled giggle, "every man should locate him some real choice brush, I always say."

In the hardware drawer the boy searched out the short, hooked brush knife and a sliver of whetstone, and from under the sink took two apples and one of the folded burlaps sacks. He placed the apples and knife and whetstone in the sack along with a book of matches picked up from the table. As he knotted the sack he looked at the pile of beer cans and wondered how a man could drink that much beer and keep those kind of habits and still wake

up in the morning looking like an ad for toothpaste. "With probably not more'n two hours sleep—" *It aint right; hawks ought to
have spines and fangs; woodducks ought to look like toads . . .*
The last flatcar passes; he steps onto the track and watches that
car crash away, cursing after it. The track turns and the train
is consumed by the forest, sound and all, as suddenly as it came.
The track, still furred with soft red rust, shows no sign that a
train ever passed. He proceeds on down the other side of the
embankment, toward the motionless dance of junk. "—and with
a good two days worth of whiskers to boot . . . like a goddamn
toothpaste ad."

[II.]        SPRING  RAIN

by

Ken Kesey

The rain fell, splitting and hissing through the great stacked
ranks of pine needles. It had started so fast the sun was still
shining. He ran, holding the spray of huckleberry over his head,
thinking that if it hadn't been for that damn car, if it just hadn't
been for that damned old car.

He ran out of the woods and toward the tracks. Across the tracks
he could see the little tarpaper shed where he would find shelter.
The sun wasn't shining anymore and it rained harder. Before he
could cover the fifty yards from the abrupt edge of the woods to
the tracks, a little logging train squealed and came down off the
hill and cut him off from the shack. He could see his shelter flash
between the ends of the great shaggy logs as the cars went by. He
stood at the edge of the tracks and cursed it as it went by, and when
it was gone he threw down his spray of leaves and proceeded

31

slowly on toward the shack, because he was already completely wet.

Inside the shack he set on a keg and unbottoned his shirt. The shack was still warm from the April sun, and it smelt of warm tarpaper and pitch. At the door of the shack the rain fell so hard that it looked like a shimmering celophane curtain, and on the tarpaper roof it sounded like a thousand panicked people running, running.

He had hung his shirt on a nail and was unbuttoning his pants when he saw the girl come through the rain curtain. He knew her first name was Clarice but he didn't know her last. He had her in his literature class. She was tall, so tall that she always appeared to feel obvious and embarrassed, and her face was long. In class he had always thought that she looked like she was about to break into tears and run from the room. Only now she stood just inside the doorway shaking her hands and laughing. In one of her hands she carried a short hooked brush knife exactly like the one he carried. She had not seen him at the back of the shack yet and started to unbutton the top of her dress.

"Any old port in a storm," he said.

She was very startled. "Who's that."

"Just me. I got caught out in it too and came running for this shed."

"Oh. Oh, you're Will Strafford. Hello."

"Hi." He wondered why she had been laughing and asked her. She appeared embarrassed and angry.

"I was not laughing," she said.

"Well, it sure looked like it. I didn't know you cut brush."

She was further embarrassed and angry. She turned her back on him and looked back out through the rain to the woods. "I don't, usually. I didn't know you cut either."

"I don't either, usually," he told her. Each knew the other was lying. All the high school kids cut brush to sell to the florists along the coast, but none of them liked to admit it. "I was just doing it to get some money to fix up my car."

"You don't even have a car. You're not old enough."

"I'm sixteen. And I have a Ford."

For some reason he wanted to cry out. He wanted to curse, the girl, the rain, the car, the whole world. Everything is so goddamned miserable, he thought. He hated everything. He hated the girl, and he hated the way they had to talk to each other. It wasn't just because she wasn't one of the bunch because it wouldn't have made any goddamned difference. If she'd been one of the bunch they would have talked about one of the bunch, and what the bunch was doing. And they would have talked and talked the rain out and felt uncomfortable and miserable and so goddamned terribly sad. It wouldn't have made any difference.

For fifteen minutes it rained and they were silent, angry and hurt with each other. It was so terribly painful and sad that they both wanted to cry. The thousand crazy panicky feet still beat madly on the roof, and the wind jumped into the line of green-grey pines. The shack grew colder and he could see her start to shiver.

"C'mon back here," he said, "It's a little warmer. Look. I can put this plank across these kegs and make a crazy bench."

She looked at him hostilely but came back and set down on his bench. She set all bent forward in her wet clothes, like a wet bird. Her hands were clasped around the knife, and she bent over it, between her knees. Her face was very sad and very wet, and he thought she might have been crying.

"Hey, old Miss Crawford is really a creep, isn't she?" Miss Crawford was their literature teacher, a little humpbacked woman who had a habit of whispering into a disorder, "Be sweet, now children, be sweet."

The girl looked over at him and this time he was sure she was going to break into sobs. "I like Miss Crawford," she said, but she didn't cry.

"Yeah, I guess she's all right. Just goofy, you know?"

He leaned forward and wrapped his arms about himself. He was shivering a little now, and he could feel the chill start to raise bumps on his skin. They set for a sit, like wet chickens on a roost. Then between his feet the boy noticed a tiny bloom growing up through the floorboards of the shack, like a tiny white three-cornered star. He reached down and picked it and it was so fragile and delicate on its pale stem that he felt somehow chosen and special in just finding it.

"A trillium," he said, "The first one I've seen this year. It's just bloomed, just today, see how the petals are still bent in?"

She had set up and was looking at the little flower so sadly that he felt sorry that he'd picked it. But picking the flower was the way things are, just something you do because it's there, and then with it in your hand and your hand trying to be careful and easy and preserve the beauty and freshness of it that is already destroyed, that was destroyed the minute that the careful hand reached down and snapped off its line to life, you start to feel miserable again.

"Here," he said, and pushed the bloom at her, "Want it?"

She took his hand in both of hers and pressed flower and hand to her cheek. He was so surprized at her action that he couldn't speak. When he turned on the bench to face her she was looking into his eyes. Her face and hair were still wet, and her lips felt very cold when he kissed her. He was thinking, she'll give herself to me if I want her. Right here in this old shed. She'll really do it, too. She must have been in love with me for a long time. Jesus, really in love with me.

He pulled her urgently to him and could feel her sobbing. He felt tremendously excited, and was thinking very hard, trying to preserve every little bit of it for the remembering and the telling later. Over her shoulder on the floor he saw the little flower where it had fallen crushed in the eagerness of their embrace. He thought harder than ever to fix each movement and each word and each sensation, and on the tarpaper overhead the thousand panicked feet rattled in pointless and miserably frenzy.

[III.]     SPRING  RAIN

by

Ken Kesey

The rain fell. Not from the sky overhead for the sky was clear polished blue, but from the direction of the abrupt green wall of mountains. Not even falling if you came right down to it, but being blown in a stinging slant from the clouds across the mountains, clouds you couldn't even see.

It didn't seem hardly fair, he thought. Getting drenched under a blue sky.

Fair or not the rain blew into the narrow coastal valley with a sound so vicious it seemed to be cursing between its silvered teeth. It hissed through the shiny green pine needles and trembling scrub oak; it slashed through the blackberry vines and salmon-berry vines and huckleberry bushes; its anger finally exhausted, it fell in quick drips from the fern, to the sheep sorrel, to the grass, and eventually to the invisible earth hiding beneath the green jungle.

The sun was still shining, like a ball of wet gold foil, but it offered no warmth. The wind drove the rain like nails. He ran through forest with his head down, holding a thick, flat spray of huckleberry over his head like an umbrella and cursing as he ran.

"Jesus Christ, man. There aint a cloud in the sky, not a motherin' cloud. Even a blue sky will for Christ sake take advantage of you."

When he reached the wire fence at the edge of the woods the sun was no longer shining. Across the railroad tracks was a small logging camp abandoned last fall; a scatter of broken buildings and weird, ungainly machinery that dribbled rust into the grass; broken crates, twisted boiler pipes, cogs with missing teeth, an old boot with its tongue dripping—this solemn and purposeless clutter performed a solemn and purposeless dance about the tall, thin spar tree that stood in the center of the clearing, moored there by dozens of cables and old ropes that fluttered like crepe in the wind. It was the first day of May.

Climbing the fence he could see the little tarpaper shed beneath the spar where he would find shelter. He dropped from the fence into a snarl of berryvine that filled the ditch along the track like green steel wool three feet deep; before he could fight his way through this tangle to the tracks a logging train screamed and charged from the forest to cut him off. He climbed from the vines and stood at the edge of the track, close enough to the rusty wheels of the train that he could see red drops appearing on the backs of his hands and his arms as the train swirled rusty water on him. He stood with his shoulders cupping inward about his chest and cursed the train as it went by. He could see the tarpaper roof of the shack flash between the ends of the great shaggy logs as the cars banged past . . . standing, with a small hooked knife in one hand and that spray of flat leaves in the other, he cursed each car as it came before him, forlornly and steadily, as if he were reading the white stenciled words from the side of each flatcar as it went past.

He had lived along this part of the Oregon Coast all his sixteen years; a sudden rain in May, a cold wind, a logging train that cut off shelter—none of these things should have surprised or upset him. Not in this country, he thought; not this mothering month.

But it wasn't the month, it was the year. This whole year had been uncomfortable and sour. Everything seemed to annoy him in a way he couldn't explain. He knew it was more than the rain. He'd been angry and uncomfortable all morning in a sun that made the wet forest a mountain of emeralds. He decided it was his old man, lushed out in the kitchen again last night with some honky tonk from Waconda. He decided that was the cause of it.

He hadn't wanted to be around when they got up so he had left the house early, before the sun had burned off the low ground fog, and had sneaked off on his bicycle. Not to keep from waking his father—the old man wouldn't be up until the woman booted him out about noon for a ride home—but to keep from waking that noisy girl next door. He carried a bundle of burlap strips and a short hooked knife tied to the handle bars as he rode toward the big state park that lay between the town and the mountains. As he rode it grew lighter. By the time he had hidden his bicycle at the edge of the park and started up the railroad the sun had burned off most of the fog and the rain-wintered ties under the tracks were steaming. White sign at the edge of the park: "WACONDA AUGA STATE PARK. Picking or combing of brush punishable by fine or imprisonment." He walked a half mile past the sign, up the tracks, then turned out of sight into the dense brush. He worked cutting fern and huckleberry sprays with his hooked knife, for two hours, cutting them with a quick upward jerk then tying the sprays in the burlap strips when he had four dozen and stacking the bundles by a tall, bare snag he had noted so he could come back that night and haul them out and sell the bundles to a florist-and-undertaker in Waconda who would know the bundles came from the state park but who wouldn't say anything because the combings from the park were the best. He had been the one, in fact, that had suggested to the boy that he could get better cuttings from the park. "Ain't that illegal?" the boy had asked. The florist-and-undertaker lifted his eyebrows and shrugged. "You think I'm Dick Tracy? I pay ten dollars for the bundles you cut out of the brush; I pay maybe twenty dollars for the bundles you bring from the park."

The boy had cut and tied six bundles when the wind had blown the rain over the mountains onto him. Now he wondered why he hadn't brought them with him when he'd made his run for shelter. He threw in a couple of curses at himself for forgetting, barely breaking his rhythm as he cursed the train. His flat, disconnected voice joined with the whirling clatter of the train wheels to make a sound not without melody.

When the train was past he stepped onto the track and watched the last car crash away, disappearing as suddenly as it had come. The track turned and the train was consumed by the forest. Even the sound of it gone, absorbed by wet leaves and moss. The rain fell. The tracks showed no sign that the train had ever been there. They were still rusty. He proceeded slowly down the embankment and through the motionless dance of junk to the shack under the spar.

Inside the shack he sat down on a keg and unbuttoned his shirt. The shack was still warm from the morning sun, and it smelled of warm tarpaper and pitch. At the door the rain fell so hard that it looked like a shimmering curtain of glass beads. On the tarpaper roof it roared as if a thousand panicked animals were stampeding over his head. He hung his shirt on a nail and began kicking apart one of the kegs. Nails scattered, still shining because someone had thought to pour crankcase oil into the kegs last fall.

"Well," he said, looking down at the burst keg. "Well, what the hell anyhow? So it's nails." He began kicking the keg again, methodically, until the wood was completely splintered and the nails were all over the floor. He piled up the broken staves on the dirt floor and struck a match to them. They started quickly, giving off any oily black smoke at first. He coughed and cursed the fire. The oil burned out of the staves and the fire stopped smoking. He took off his pants and hung them near the fire, on a tripod he made of some old quarter-rounds (why hadn't he used those instead of the nail keg?). He was bent shivering over the fire when he saw the girl through the rain curtain; poised, stooped, with a wet and baffled air . . . standing between a boiler pipe and a big, quaking fan wheel, as if she had joined the dance. He walked to the doorway and started to call, then went back and put on his steaming pants. He hid his brush knife and returned to the door.

"Hey out there. Come on in. I got a fire going. Come on in, for Christ sake; what's the matter with you out there?"

It irritated him the way she turned and walked quickly to the shack with her head down and her arms at her side. She hadn't been startled at all to find she was being watched. She stopped just inside the door and wiped strands of wet hair from her face with the back of a hand that held a knife like his. He wasn't at all surprised to see that it was the girl from next door.

"Well, what you say, Clarice?" He rubbed his hands over the fire.

"Who's that?" she said, but still had not looked up. Her hand touched her wet hair then travelled to the top of her dress and fumbled with the button there. Who, he wondered, would wear a *dress* brush cutting?

"It's me," he said. "I got caught out in it too and came running for this shed. Any old port, you know."

"Oh. Oh, Joe Ben Stamper."

"Yeah. Joe Stamper. We live next door."

"Oh . . . hi." She had not moved farther into the shack toward him. She stood with one fidgeting hand plucking at her hair and her dress, pinching a piece of the wet cloth occasionally and pulling it out from her skin. She was tall, so tall that in school she was kidded by the boys and called "Spar Pole." Her eyes were always closed or opened wide as if she were startled to discover herself up so high. The boy nodded at the knife she held:

"I didn't know you snuck into the park to cut brush," he said

"I don't, usually," she said, flaring angry and embarrassed. "I didn't know *you* cut illegal brush, either."

His shrug was intended to indicate that it made not the slightest difference to him. "I'm not Dick Tracy," he said. "I'm just out getting some bread to fix up my ol' car."

"You don't even have a car. You're not old enough."

"Like hell! I'm sixteen. I bought my cousin Hank's thirty-nine Merk when Hank went in the Navy. Damn it, you know that. It's been sitting in the yard for a week."

"Oh?" she said, irritating him more than ever. "I was under the impression that car belonged to one of your father's friends. He seems to have so many come visiting him."

He shrugged again, prodding the fire. She changed her approach.

". . . besides, you are not sixteen."

"Well, I guess I know what I am. I guess I didn't fail the third grade which makes me a year older'n the rest of the class huh? Hell."

"You're not very big for sixteen."

"Jesus H. Christ!" he yelled. "I'm just as big as any one of the other guys. Just because I'm no mothering six foot freak like you."

He yelled at her across the little shack, angry at her, angry at the very sound of his voice against the rain. He was angry because her being a girl restricted his anger, limited him to shouting; if she'd been a boy they would have fought. He wanted to fight her, to strike her with something. He wanted to run out of the shack, even back into the damned rain. He felt a tight, swelling rage building in his chest, a thwarted fury. He began to curse at the standing form, as he had cursed the flatcars passing, as he would sometimes lie in his bed and curse the noise crashing from his father's room through their thin walls . . . words to relieve the terrible swelling that had been building and building in him.

The girl didn't seem hurt by the barrage. The curses were without heat, rolling out like magic incantations. New-learned adolescent words he had practiced alone, new combinations of words, pouring forth in the little shack with the rhythm of a religious chant. When the chant had no effect on the girl he turned it on the rain, on the town and the school and the woods and his father and everything, naming one thought after another and cursing it as it came through his mind, roaring through his mind with clicking, spattering wheels . . . cutting him off, leaving him to stand in the rain, cut off.

The thoughts finally roared past and he became quiet. He looked up at the lowered face of the tall girl; her eyes were closed, her head bowed. She stood as if she were in church, listening to the benediction. Looking at her it suddenly occurred to him that she had followed him out here; how else could they have met in this vast, dense park?

"Hey, Clarice . . . hey. C'mon back here. It's a little warmer by the fire. Look, I can put these planks across two kegs and make a bench."

She glared hostilely at him but came back and set down on the bench he constructed. She sat with her hands closed at her throat, bent forward in her blue dress. Like a wet bird, he thought, like one of them blue herons on a log. Bending forward there with that

39

rusty brush knife held under her chin like a beak. Like one of them big winged herons that flies to music . . .

He stood up. "Hey, I'll kick another keg apart and build up the fire."

"No," she said. "it's all right. I'm all right. Don't destroy their kegs."

"Hell. It's just loggers. It's the company's kegs anyway. The loggers don't give a damn. Nobody cares."

"You still shouldn't . . ."

"Jeez, you're really a case, really a nut. Don't you think if some logger from the company was wondering around cold and he found some kegs and they belonged to me, don't you think he'd kick 'em apart for firewood?"

"He might, but that's no reason for you to—"

"That's a reason for everybody." He began kicking at the keg. "It's the golden rule."

He pulled the broken staves from the oily nails and laid them on the fire. There was black smoke for a time, and she coughed. Where he sat there was less smoke and he wanted to trade places with her, but he didn't. They were quiet for a time, like wet birds at each end of a roost. Then the girl noticed a tiny bloom growing up through the dirt floor of the shack, a flower like a tiny, white, three-cornered star . . .

"A trillium," she said. "The first one I've seen this year. It's just bloomed, just today. See how the petals are still bent in?"

He reached out and picked the flower and held it toward her with a comical sweeping of his hand; "It's yours," he said grandly.

"Why, thank you sir," she laughed and took the hand that held the flower and pressed her lips to it. Then crushed flower and hand to her cheek. As he let her rub her cheek against the back of his hand he observed an interesting phenomena taking place within him: his brain had begun to calculate. Of it's own accord it started down a path of cunning and planning. He observed it thinking: *she'll let you. You can take her. That's what she came out here for. You can take her. Right here in this old shed. She's been after you a long time if you'll just think back. All you have to do is play it casual, go slow, take it easy. Just the way they do in the mysteries, just the way the guys tell about it. A little bit at a time. Play it slow and you can put it to her right here yesman!*

He watched his brain work, marvelled at it. It did not even seem

to be his. It was anybody's, everybody's but his. He had no say
over it. It was tremendously excited, this brain, trying to plan and
at the same time record and perserve every little bit for the telling
later: her wet hair; her wet lips; the tears and the rain; his hand
slipping down her cheek to the buttons of her wet dress, feeling
the cold, firm crown of her breast over the top of her bra. Yes
man, it was something! He watched, and watched himself watching—a trick with two mirrors—without letting his brain know he
was watching, or what he was going to do. "Joe Ben, Joe Ben,"
the girl breathed. His brain flashed at the words but, watching, he
was amused.

He waited a while longer, amused and peacefully content to
watch, before he finally crashed through and asserted his crossing,
and when the girl told them about it later—at the service station,
at the hospital—she said it was like he just all of a sudden for no
reason at all went crazy. She said the two of them had been sitting
quietly waiting the rain out—he'd put his arm around her, yes,
that and a little kiss, but nothing else—when he'd all of a sudden
for no reason at all seemed to tear apart and go completely crazy.
He began to scream and hit at her, tear at her clothes and kick at
her (she had the marks to prove it) and threaten all kinds of
things. Yes, she told them, he knew I had the knife, he'd said
something about it. No, she told them, he didn't act worried about
it or try to take it away. Even after he must have known I was
going to have to use it.

She cried and they told her it was alright, he was just cut up a
little and wouldn't die. "His face, though," she said, and cried.

The doctor gave her a shot and her parents drove her home to
bed. Through the rain of her bedroom window she could see his
old car rusting on the shaggy yard. The light on the wet hood, the
wash of water on her window pane, the shot the doctor had given
her . . . made her think the car was leaned forward in an attitude
of fantastic speed as it stood there. She fell asleep wondering if it
would be gone in the morning.

\*      \*      \*

## Notes on a night in Florence:

I go to see the Dows with Ruth Ashton. We see them at dinner through the windows. Ruth knocks loud. Deaf. The old man comes to the door. Much shouting. Ruth and old man too much alike—talk, hold the stand is the important thing; never mind what is said. Ruth leaves after a blurred, shouting introduction.

The old woman has white hair pinched in a bun. Her body seems obscene and nude beneath her dress, probably because it has sagged and shrunken and leaves the bony protrusions thrusting against the flowered material. Dress a nondescript pattern, the same unnoticed pattern on old women everywhere. Probably flowers. She has a towel safety pinned about her narrow shoulders like a shawl. Why? It's warm in the house; why a shawl? Maybe as you grow old your body begins to cool towards death. The old man had on a sweater also. Yet, I was warm.

The old woman's eyes were fretfull, distracted, unfocussed behind spectacles. She gave me coffee and a sugar cookie from a celophane sack. The oven was full of kindling. They were eating cold cereal from blue bowls. The old man apologized for the meagerness of their dinner, saying they eat a big lunch in the afternoon. I believed his story, but why should it be necessary for him to tell me this? He is still afraid a person will think poorly of him if he is poor.

In fact, the whole impression was one of apology. The bragging he did was a sad, inward bragging like I used to hear in the hospital; the bragging of a small man.

The old woman's knuckles were big as golf balls. The old man (and woman too, I recall) moved suddenly fast at first, then caught themselves and slowed as if remembering the age of their bodies, as if their bodies reminded them they were not as young as I.

Their talking overlapped. Before the man would finish a phase the woman had interrupted, being reminded somewhere in the man's speech of something, she would come on with new vigor and energy and after a few seconds the man would concede and hush. Then he would be reminded of something by her speech and start up, finally drowning her out. Neither ever finished what they were saying. There was an animosity present in these inter-changes, but it was old and worn and died out quickly.

The house was an amazing clutter. Whatever was finished with laid where it had fallen. It looked like a house of an old bachelor. Like Jess's old cabin. Everything flat held an object. The mantle, the windowsills, the one overstuffed chair, the tables all covered with clothes, books, newspapers. Their mantle held books, empty patent medicine bottles, a carnival clock of a horse dipped in gold, boxes of snuff, bottles of water holding rocks from Arizona, magazines, an old radio, a model of a rocking chair, maps, photographs . . . everything that had some iota of sentimental value.

From the door frame hung some manner of harness, white canvas and chairs and straps. The old man had fallen from the roof a few months ago and broke some ribs. This must have been for his use.

The old woman brought out a box of sea shells and coral sent to them by their son in the Coastguard in "the phill . . the phil . . near . . . . . . . . . in Pearl Harbor." Her smooth fingers felt the old shells. Her fingers seemed to have had the blood drawn from them. The skin was too much for the meat it contained.

The old man brought a oddly shaped stone that he thought must be a "painting stone." The Indians held it between their legs and ground up dyes in it. He was probably right. He gave me this head sized chunk of rock to hold and another piece half the size of it. I sit there, wondering how to hold both.

The old man gets a sudden idea about something I should "get in my mind" and heads off to locate it in the clutter, forgets after a few minutes search what he is looking for. The old woman points out pictures on the wall, ancient shots of long gone rock formations, and then shows me photos in the newspaper of heli-copters placing telephone poles. The old man hands me a stone from a river in Yellowstone park. The old woman shows me a picture from Arizona Highways.

I promise to return and practically run out the door.

\*                 \*                 \*

The notes, diagrams, character studies, etc. that follow were written by Ken Kesey for his own use. Although he often seems to be addressing someone else, invariably his audience is Ken Kesey looking over the notes at another time.

*Remember the grin* that haunts Lee.
Remember the ghost that haunts and haunts all the Stampers.

# The Arrangement

Let's take a look at my plot: okay so far we got this clear: Lee is come home to do Hank Harm: There he finds a plot already in progress. Hank is selling lumber to W.P. and the people are beginning to hassle him about it. He sticks to his guns through terrific pressure, from the town, from the elements, from Viv and Lee, but gives in when Joe Ben dies. Then changes his mind when he goes to visit old Henry and sees Henry is shot down by Jonas —Hank finds out then that the old man has known all along, but figured what the hell, Hank needed a mother and did the best he could—then Boney has to tell about Hank giving in. Hank sees how it effects people when he gives in, Lee sees also, sends Viv back.

It's a good plot, it seems now. To tighten it just make sure everyone is aware of what is at stake so the conflict is increased.

And I've got good conflicts going with most of my main characters. I think plotwise it's pretty strong.

Now about this business with the words: wouldn't it be easier to turn the mind to one task at a time and quit worrying about so many. As I rewrite I'm trying for effect with arrangement and interwoven P.V., something to give the reader more than one eye, this is going to be tough enough. I should devote most of this time through to that. To arrangement alone. I've got plenty techniques now for prisming the P.V., all of which need polishing badly, so I don't need to continue experimenting, at least not in the time left me, I should go right on through as quickly as possible, all the way through, in fact, before I do any more yellowpage work, and saving enriching the vocabulary for a later stage. I'm trying to block in and tend to detail all at once.

I have plenty going. I should get what bones I have created firmly in place the way I want them before I begin fleshing in the details. This will require some discipline and some scheduling of deadlines. You're moving much too slowly because you're expending too much power in too many directions and are therefore diluting the whole output on all points. If I went through this thing for word richness alone I would be doing a better job than I am now by far, same with humor. Didn't I add much of the humor last in *Cuckoo*? The monopoly scene.

So I must hold off a little on these other things. I could go through once reading one mentor, go through a second reading another and so on, but first I must have the arrangement.

I think I have visualised my technique, cleared up the doubt and made it easier for myself as well as the reader:

It will run like this with the mainstream

going until such a time when we, the author, can

call in another of Voices he thinking ... then

when that peters out naturally back to

the regular — but I have established to the reader who said it and what his speech looks like

in a natural way — so the next time I use italics he is going to know [learning as I did] that such simplicity was difficult to come by & etc and then back. Then to have somebody speak in quotes in parenthesis ("If you got to know, compadres, how it works.") and we can then let these three wander off, to be swung in whenever most effective

(over)

then to Hondo & so forth.

back, something happening in 3rd person illuminate

switch into italics this time knowing it will

be away, knowing also that you my come back

Yet there should be something corrected if at all possible

to another. Quaint parentheses go on longer, begins to

stray so the jump back to 3rd person is clean, but.

still easy to get back

again Lee in italics, only the Lee the connection is not quite

so strong nor want 'by and quite so pertinent to the

story 3rd person is telling'

a pertinent quote in parenthesis occurs

back easily to 3rd person, as usually happens, leaving italics

mentions something Lee thinks, printed in italics

straight 3rd person narrative

So, each section begins afresh and must set up a new series of transitions and stick to the rules of these up until the end. Perhaps the whole book may eventually be the same. I think that was ~~probably~~ probably my idea when I made this chart

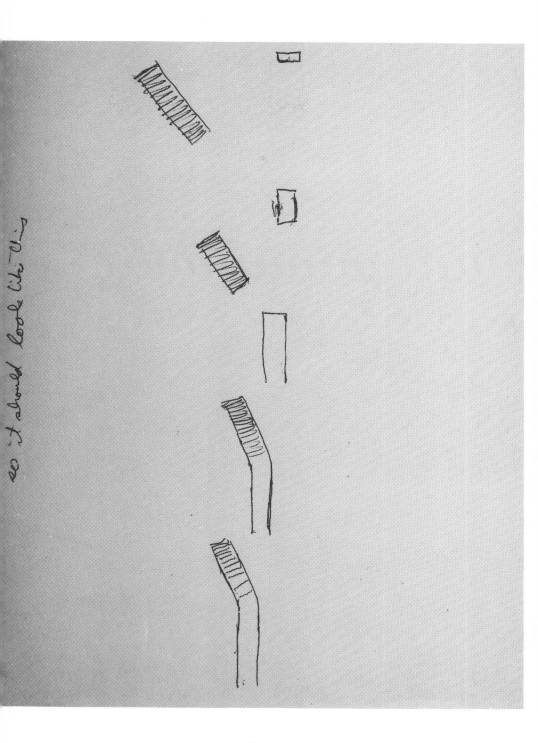

so it should look like this

I haven't settled into a method on this book yet.

I've got a lot of things going that don't fit into the feeling I want.

It's going to be hard. Maybe impossible. Maybe I'm trying too much, like in Cockoo's nest when I tried to push two things, the faces and the machinery. I resolved them and kept both, but not in the same power I first used.

I'm still groping for everything in this book. Maybe I should get style first and let plot come. I kind of think so. It'd be easier.

Style:

I have a story being told by three people, me, Hank and Lee. Lee's style will come, if I can keep it from being Arny. Hank will come if I can keep him from being Chief or McMurphy. But my style is the important one.

What do I want?

A cross between Faulkner and Burroughs and also me.

How?

*Me, Kesey, with something important* to tell *something* damned important. A *story* I already know and am going to tell just as quickly as possible. The best way would be to go through the whole book at the mind, not have it reel past on a flimsy string of narrative.

I want a sense of urgency—with the start and get a sense of intimacy and *incidently, by the way,*

The other books had urgency. I think the present tense start is the secret. See the house as it stands now.

Start with the house? But what about the Barrier? the story of the coast? Maybe start with the house, then say it stands like a guard, an outpost at a wall.

*Start with the house in the present. Give it a sense of Urgency!*

With perhaps a human leg. This is a good grabber, but what? Why? How pertinent?

I know whose leg. Old Henry's, amputated because infection set in, because he came back to work when Lee left. But what does it mean?

It's worth figuring out as a grabber, worth using if it can be more than that.

So why? and what?

Ah—a flag pole where our flags could be hoisted when the supply truck drove past. Pictures of bread or milk or a pig for pork. *When Lee arrives he might see something hanging on the pole and recall the method of ordering.*

But what does it mean to hoist the leg? *A dig at the truck driver by old Henry for his not selling them stuff because they won't join the union. That's a surface reason.* What it is, is defiance on old Henry's part. A grim humorous defiance—of what? The Union for one, joining for another. Weakness for another. Make something between old Henry and the driver so he can really hate. They are old friends, old friends, old arguers. One of their arguments is Conservative strong will against the welfare state (old age, unions, pensions). And it shows old Henry still standing on his one leg.

But back to style.

Now, if we start with that we are going to tell why that leg is up there and what it means. The reader has something to expect.

I like it; a leg hanging by its foot. It makes a good start for the book; also a good symbol, the type of thing that would appear anywhere and people would associate it with the book.

Still, how can it tie in more strongly with "Sometimes I get a great notion to jump into the river and drown?"

Perhaps an arm instead, tied around the wrist as the hand seems to be gripping the rope. Holding itself out of the water, the hand gripping as though it would climb out of the water.

Now . . . . this arm will give me a *reason*. My reason is to tell about it.

This will give my style.

So, I start with the house, then the arm, then the barrier of mountains if I can work them in (maybe not-maybe Lee can think it, or Hank on a drive over the hills). Then the history of the stricken house. (this not like ordinary exposition but as an exploration of why the house is out on its peninsula).

*So the book is on the surface a long exploration of the arm.* And *why* someone would hang such a symbol of defiance.

The impression given by the hanging arm is one of defiance because of the house's grim defiance. It would be different if it was on a different house, but from this great stubborn tombstone it is defiant.

So this because it leads me to tell why the house happens to be built as it is.

*And everything has to have bearing on that arm's being there.* Everything leads to the hanging of it.

The knot around the arm could be cut away—the arm wouldn't fall.

How about the finger? Dast I?

*This means that the whole community is in on it. The whole bunch wants them to unionize so the strike will end. (if they quit supplying wood, the people feel, the strike will end. They sell wood to one big operation; this operation owns most of the mills as long as it can get wood it's okay).* It doesn't want to pay the wage jump. No, not wage jump—*guaranteed yearly wage with benefits.* As long as the Stricker mill can furnish a certain amount they can keep going—if it drops below that amount they'll have to meet the union's demand. The town doesn't know all this at first, so they aren't so unfriendly toward the slickers.

(I'm going to change the name to Stamper.)

So, after the operation the truck driver calls (no, he calls after the townspeople contact old Henry and try to push him into joining) and tells Henry he'll resume service, Henry, *Takes the arm from the freezer and bends down the fingers and hangs it there* for all to see and know—it's like Patton saying "Nuts" to a surrender request.

" . . . . and wonder about the *family* that would hang up an arm."

So, we go back to the building of the house, story of the family of Thrasher, and the story follows off after Lee because he leaves the family group—an unusual and noteworthy thing.

To Lee in Berkeley, coming home, arrival, explanation of circumstances, a week of work, the drunk in town so we have a *first section.*

Now—back to style: I tell the story fast and hard, as if it is only a story—and Hank and Lee talk it into significance. But the style must have a sense of urgency, direction and importance.

\*       \*       \*

"Sometimes I live in the country,
Sometimes I live in the town,
Sometime I get a great notion
to jump into the river and drown."

"One Flew Over the Cuckoo's Nest"
"Sometimes I Get a Great Notion

"A Great Notion"

Sometimes A Great Notion

The River... water flowing to the sea.

The river flows out to sea.

The sea is surrender. Not the sea itself. No, it is a
conquerer; it is the giving into it that is surrender.
It waits. It doesn't wait. It tears at the
land, at life & mankind. It grows away our
coast lines and smoothes out our mountains.

We made it up out of the sea, stormed around
on land for a time, now the sea is bent on
reclaiming us.

Because we have failed, or are failing. You can't
stop on land. the sea will get you.

53

The sea is always after you. The rains tear building away.

The water is death. Not dead, death.

To jump into the river is to submit to death, to watery nothingness.

Yet... Sometimes I get this great notion,

To give up, and return to death, to nothingness, to nothing.

The sea is mother - to return to the mother is death. To return to the sea is death.

Perhaps... even to return is death, to return anywhere.

~~The~~

We start with this boy, 21-24, returning after learning enough to lose God. God is no more for him. He would like there to be God, heaven, hell. Goblins Ghosts devils. Anything. That would give his ~~life~~ life meaning. With the rules and the reward gone, so is meaning.

He returns and must find a choice. The Water. Death. Dark, meaningless silence on the one hand.
And something else on the other hand.

54

Let me see how much of the plot I already know:

Father has beat a logging operation out of the wilderness. Now is grown old. Can't hold up his end. His oldest son is Foreman. His youngest lives in San Francisco with his divorced wife.

No one but relatives work for him. Why? To keep the Union off of his back. Being relatives he can make them partners of some sort and keep out of the union.

The Union: The answer, yet not the answer. The labor Union is like the sea, the river; it, to the father, is surrender, death.

The loss of identity in a great amorphous.

Which is what drowning in the sea is.

So... when the father takes sick there is only one relative left: Younger son, down in San Francisco. They send for him.

When the word arrives it is right after he has lost everything and decided to kill himself — or decided, rather, to die.

His return is a return to die ... it might take him a year, or 60 years, but he too has accepted death.

He arrives and moves in with Big brother and his wife. We get the three main characters: Big brother the winner, the fighter, the strong.

Little brother: the loser, the weak.

And the girl: Something else. I haven't figured yet exactly what else.

Big brother believes: you fight. you struggle, you don't give up, you don't let down, you don't accept death.

During the time there little brother falls in love with the wife:

His conflict: how to reconcile love with death.

He attracts her and makes her love him because of his helplessness and weakness. He needs desperately. B.B. doesn't. The wife loves him but can see she is needed more by L.B.

Big Brothers conflict: winning has always been the way to success. Now he sees his strength and his winning defeating him. The way to keep his wife is to be weak.

Night—a candle, a joint—wind coming against the window in unexpected wet charges.

I'll be LEE for a while—and look at the world, the way Chuck and I used to do talking, our long days and preludin.

I don't want to sacrifice my book to prose, character or plot—the more important thing must show through which is . . . . . ?
STORY

How to get around meaninglessness.

I'll try this like Burroughs says for a while let the mind take its time—there's a plenty.

Lee should see things in terms, the way Bromden did in terms of his combine. This ties together the metaphors. What would Lee's combine be? *A ticker tape of dying, a manufacturer of robot identities bent on death,* an outside yet inside thing.

Outside in that he is out there laughing. Who? The un-thing, the vacuum, *the grinning space between the stars, the metal laughter of night, the great grinning cities* . . .

What? Death, oblivion (that's it) *oblivion,* nothing, a *nothing with a sense of humor—like the cheshire cat which had disappeared except for his grin.*

Somehow this is evident—*insisting* from objects about you (remember the chief!) A thermometer covered with vaseline was charged with pertinent significance. *A stone ticks.* (Time) *The hand of a clock reaches out to deliver a judo chop.*

Time, *death bed is an open grave.*

\*　　　　　\*　　　　　\*

Lee enters the house.

Action first, see later. The old man rising rocking stamping across the floor. "By god, by god." Happy and surprised. Here is just what he needs, just after the union man left.

He shakes Lee's hand with his left hand, moving, shouting, calling into parts of the house he can't see to fix Leland Stanford some lunch. How long you been on the road, boy?

Lee thinks, this old incredible conglomeration of smell and plaster is my father.

So old he has begun to petrify—half of him dirty yellow limestone and the other half refusing to lie down and give up. Lee meets, remeets Joe Nathan, the son of your uncle John, dead now. Joe Nathan is somewhere near Hank's age. A shy, young seeming man given to blushing. His wife is in the hospital at the moment, awaiting the birth of his first baby.

Roaring, stomping exhileration. The old man recharged. Shouting off for Viviane. Hank telling him to cool yourself, you old fart. You'll bust everything you've got. The old man furious at this, cursing Hank calling him a snotnose, telling him to wait until he gets this cast off his arm; he'd tear into him now but might hurt him all armored like he is.

Lee thinks. It's all some kind of skit they've been performing for years with no variations.

Lee is surprised by the number of rooms. He doesn't remember the house being this big. He doesn't remember it as any size at all. It was a place, like a hospital or a schoolhouse an establishment of corridors and rooms that isn't thought of in terms of size. Hank tells him the old man has probably added some rooms since he left—he's always sticking a room on one place or the next.

Hank says this looks like an empty one. (indicating that there are always an undetermined number of relatives here—maybe Joe Ben's wife is in one of these rooms) and it is Lee's old room. Both are aware of this. And next to it was his mother's room. Where Lee had watched Hank make love to his mother. Hank and Lee are both aware of this also.

When Hank leaves Lee goes to the hole and is surprised that it hasn't been covered. He looks in. It is no longer a bedroom. It is a sewing room and study. And Lee sees a girl is at the window (the room was given his mother because it afforded a good view of the river)—Hank when he leaves Lee, says he'd like to hang around but he has to take the launch on up to the mill—old Henry down like this means lots of extra work. Lee is in the room when he hears the launch leave. He goes to the hole and looks in and sees Viviane enter and stand at the window looking out on the river after the disappearing boat. He watches her, noting the melancholy, dreamlike trance of the girl—an unusual beauty— face of a sleep walking beauty, lips parted—eyes huge and without focus.

Then Lee goes to lie on the bed and sleep, wondering why he is behaving like a pawn in a game that has already been played— moved by faces beyond him—back to the game now after an interruption. His life in California only a recess in the game knowing now that it was inevitable that he come back to finish what he is irrevocably involved in. Twelve years just an instant respite. Now back with the people and the place he is truly involved in and can't be done with until that game which was in progress at his leaving is finished and over with. He sleeps, wondering about the next move.

So we have some new things going. Lee as a child watched Hank screw his mother in the room next to his. Hank knew he was being watched—couldn't help but know with all the sound and racket and one day where he found the little hole was angry and took the dresser—the hole was near the dresser, bored with a patient pocketknife—and reversed the mirror so whoever would would be looking would see his own eye looking back. So, again, though nothing was said, nothing would ever be said, they both were aware of the other's knowing.

So Lee is coming home to take Hank's wife, as Hank, Lee feels, took his mother.

So we have a hate working between the two of them. Lee lets his hate be known, never realizing that his mother might have meant more to Hank than just another lay in the hay.

We learn all of this in the course of the action (i/e Lee finds a picture of his mother one time in Hank's wallet)

So what have we got going?

(sometimes at dusk it is the sky that looks solid, and the trees only torn holes in it.)

Lee and his good buddy. A life that seems unreal and unimportant to him (though he knows it should not be). Death its only outcome. A game going on in which he is the loser, feels he is the loser, and only plays out of hate, to see how much trouble he can make for his opponent.

Hank is involved in a game also, but his is with the river. (so is Lee's if he would admit it.) Lee thinks the grinner that haunts his sleep is Hank, but it is more than that.

After Lee sleeps we should go to Hank, and into his PV [point of view], picking up the "I was tickled to see old Lee." It is dark and he is bringing the launch back from the mill. I want to get him involved with his battle with the river immediately. Maybe he doesn't stay at the mill but goes on to the slopes to look for slides —time to think over the new turn of events.

(Viv—playing god—brings the runt pup to nurse along—like she helps Lee) Hank likes the way the powerful motor chews the water, the way the launch tears apart the surface, rips it open to show what the river is truely like underneath. He wonders why Lee came back, wonders as he works on the foundation around the house

Conflict? Let's get it moving . . . . . .

("S'matter that pup? Has he got anything or is he just suckin air?")

Conflict.

First: against the Union—Establish that quick, More in the first chapter—put pickets out in front of the house.

Then the subtile conflict between Lee and Hank.

\*  \*  \*

Henry felt the lovely desert despair of the perpetual fight drop icy down his belly—then he had Hank.

Jonas felt it but he never had anybody — (his wife and boys were nothing to him; he was too stiff to love) and the fear and the weakness killed him in his loneliness.

Hank never felt it. He always had the love to make him strong. First old Henry then Viv. Henry tells him this once. He feels it when old Henry begins to slip, and cousin is dead, and Viv is going to leave with Lee. Lee has never had anyone.

\*  \*  \*

60

Hank's style—is Algren's style—read Algren to write Hank *you should be able to tell a page of Hank's prose by the number of paragraphs.*

Hank's prose is *joyous. When it is sad we go into my voice. I can tell about him feeling sorry for himself.*

*Hank looks like Pan—he grins back at the fiendish no—grin of the no-god.*

Hank says "Let's *go bub; if we don't get 'im this round we'll get him the next.*

Hank shouts in the woods "Never give up."

Old Henry pounds his cast on the table and hollers. "God damn it; all I want is my fair advantage."

leit motifs or whatever

*Viv:* Thin, silent, small. Lee says, *"Like something seen out of the corner of your eye."* "A distortion of light." "A being just at the edge of our dimension." "Narrow head and great, round, unblinking eyes." "A sprite."

*Her face is white, thin, like a little slim flame at the top of a little slim candle.* A flame that can stand in a tornado and only undulate, never jerk. She seems incapable of holding still, incapable of a jerking movement. Even when she moves rapidly she has the flowing sensation of flame.

*When he sees her through the hole it is as though her face was illuminating the room.* (the light was behind her)

She is reba (should I read "Green Mansions?")

She goes with Lee and Hank duck hunting and sees the big birds that Faye saw. Hank shoots the goose and she thinks this is beautiful, to Lee's surprise—but she sympathises with Lee who sees only the violence.

*Still Viv*

What does she have that connects her to the story, to the Stampers? And the Stamper's conflict. What is the Stamper's conflict, by the way?

A restlessness, an unease in their surroundings. Do they belong? (in New England, in Kansas, in Oregon?)

The restless, uneasy, unfulfilled Stamper marries this girl who is at home in the world.

She is the one that convinces Hank the world is good and worth fighting to hold.

*When she goes outside nature seems to open to take her in as part of itself,*

Viv is a part of a mysterious world of life. Hank is the defender of that world. *Viv loves the river. Hank hates it, but respects it, and respects her love of it. But he knows she also loves the house. He must fight the river to preserve the house.*


## *Vivi* (how Hank met her)


Hank joined the navy, sailed out of San Francisco still going west. And was the first of the Stampers to complete the circle. He landed on the west coast more restless than ever. The old Stamper restlessness knowing a thwarted despair of running in a circle. He bought a cycle in the east and fled across the nation *West West*

He met a girl in a little Colorado town. Just one more in a long line. But she was different. She sized him up, liked him, and gave what he wanted because she liked him. (Later, she tells Lee she liked him because he was strong enough to be kind—a trait uncommon) When he leaves her she makes no grab to hold him. He speeds on. West. Faster and faster.

(*A Stamper has an addiction, like a waltzing mouse—the mouse killed in Lee's explosion was Myra's waltzing mouse*) to run in in a circle, convinced he is traveling in a straight line, towards something, towards whatever his blood and his Stamper bones have been seeking) *A Stamper doesn't go back.* But when Hank reached the coast he was stricken with that same anguish that had hit old Henry when he had reached the coast. *Is this the whole shebang?* Does he keep going until, like the tigers with a tail in its mouth, turning to butter beneath black Sambo? (who is the prettiest tiger in the jungle?)

He returns and convinces the girl to marry him much the way his father did. She should be somewhat wealthy and well educated.

Viv makes the huge and ominous old house (Lee remembers

it so) a home. It is her quality. When she loves, she gives; when she gives, what she has given to takes on part of her personality.

*When Lee begins taking Viv from Hank, the old Stamper restlessness comes back to Hank, like the memory of an old wind, like the wind of the notion striking his face as he cycles across country. The find full of the land, too full, the air of America.*

*The restless, unsatisfied air of America.*

## Hank    The wanderer stopped

*"Wandered in the city, wandered on the farm, all I got to show is this muscle in my arm"* . . . . . .

*He watches geese flying South, South? why never south? Why always west?*

Lee calls him Brother Loose.

He still wanders, but now, because of Viv, he has a home to return to.

He still fights, drinks, roars laughter, screws the red-bloused, blackeyed honky tonkers, roars through the sleeping Waconda on his cycle——but Viv has given him a home to return to. Something to fight for, defend. He has found the life the Stampers never found. (Lee doesn't have it. Old Henry never truly had it. He channeled his Stamper restlessness and frustration at being confronted by the sea into his logging show—so now the logging show is old Henry's life, his score, so to speak, his harvest, his bankroll, amassed by the toil of a harnessed shoulder.)

\*                    \*                    \*

## Viv:

Her character; her meaning, her story just an ordinary girl caught up in a family plot.

She almost has a child, doesn't and sort of dies with it. So?

Hank is disappointed in her and she knows this. Thinks it.

Her hair was once short. He asks that she let it grow long. Myra's was once long. Hank and Lee both are attempting to re-fashion the past, to re-work an old view. Viv is a pawn in a game, a long ago game.

She can realize this by finding the photo in the mud where the fight went on.

Then?

takes Lee away. Looking at the picture of the dead woman who would usurp her identity. Speaking to it. That photographed laugh resounded as harsh as a crow's call. She tells the picture that "We beat you. All three of us together. You tried to drag us after you but we beat you after all.

Finally confronting the woman she has spent six year trying to emulate. "You brought us together to kill us but we've beaten you."

Myra, to Viv, is a crow. Like the crows that called her to follow them into the pits of despair. Myra has *"Hair like black feathers."*

"You can't reach Hank or Lee without me, and you can't reach me without them; so we've beaten you by doing what you didn't even think any of us strong enough to do.

\*                    \*                    \*

*After the first day home:*

By this time we should know everything (almost) that went on previous to this point and be into the story.

The next day Lee is taken to the slopes. He still hasn't met Viv. He has a lunch packed for him. They try to wake him without luck. Viv has cooked breakfast but has gone (where?) *to take Joe Ben's wife into the hospital.* He gets coffee and biscuits and is hustled out to the launch. *One of the hurries is to match the upriver flow.* The launch picks up other relatives on the way. It is daylight when they reach the mill. Some of the men stay at the mill; others ride on up on the log truck, huddled here and there against the cold. *Hank tells Lee he'll have to give him a tough job right off, be-*

cause they're the easiest to learn, and Hank has no time to teach him. (Choker, some tough easy-to-explain job?) Hank leaves. Lee works. It's a job with pressure on him. He can't take his time. Hank shows back up for lunch and they eat, talk.

(The PV should, perhaps, shift to Lee when he is alone) *The lunch is significant; characteristic of Viv.* Lee notes this.

The above should move fairly fast. Lee works until near dark and rides back down on the back of the log truck, bushed completely.

*He watches Hank chopping a tree and it seems that this man is invulnerable.*

*But Lee wants a revenge. Hank knows that he does.* How does this fit in.

The whole episode should build Hank's strength in Lee's eyes, up to the last few lines when *Hank reveals his vulnerability—Viv.*

Yes Sir — *Hank has worked harder and longer than any of them. But he won't let Viv go into town to visit Joe Ben's wife; he doesn't like her crossing the river at night. He goes with Joe Ben.* Lee, *who is* too tired for supper, is awakened by this decision in the next room and watches through the hole. When Hank leaves he gets up and goes in and finally meets Viv. *He is setting about making her fall in love with him to pay Hank back for loving his mother. He does it by playing the part of the loser.*

Work the next day, harder than ever, but Lee's soreness doesn't get him until the third day and that's the day Joe Ben is gone to the hospital about his wife. Cold ride back on the boat makes him sorer than ever. He can barely move when he tells Hank he doesn't know if he can make it tomorrow or not they have a little squabble and Viv takes Lee's side.

*He has perceived her compassion for weaker animals and is using it, slowly.* Give example—pets.

He goes to work Hank tells him to buck up. It's Saturday. *Tonight we get drunk and tomorrow we sleep. The rains will come before long and no more work. Chop wood while the sun shines.*

Joe Ben shows up that afternoon and announces he has a son and they all knock off for a trip to the city. Lee learns of Hank's marital arrangement. A scene in the bar in town. Lee asks to leave early, says Hank can ride home with Joe Ben. The indication is that he is going to see Viv.

(*at the bar remember the Union hassle—keep that going.*)

As Lee leaves Hank looks after him, not so fooled as Lee

thought. He has a fair idea what is happening, but makes no move
to interfere.

Lee with Viv.

*( oh a note when the light is off in Lee's room and on in the other
room there is a thin beam on the bed. Lee realizes that this is probably how Hank found out about his peeping on him and his mother. When Hank peeks the beam is cut off and Lee is aware that
someone is looking through the hole.)*

Lee with Viv:

No sex yet—maybe. Is it too soon. No. Viv is the sort of girl who
would not be coy once committed. Make it more than a week. Let
there be a scene at breakfast that morning about working on Sat-
urdays. More affection building between Lee and Viv.

When Lee comes home he takes the boat (he has ridden the
cycle home) and tows the rowboat over with it. (This the second
week) *He'll go get anyone who honks, But this is a safeguard,*
like a locked door. No—when he leaves Hank tells him to tow
the rowboat back across so they'll have transportation. Lee doesn't
do this. He enters the house and wanders through it. He is certain
all he'll have to do is go up and find Viv. He hesitates, has a beer
in the kitchen. He sees Hank's clothes in a pile where Hank
shucked them off in his rush to get into town. (at the bar Hank
mentions leaving his wallet in his other clothes—borrows money
from Joe Ben.) Lee sees the wallet and absently picks it up. There
is a picture of Viv—Lee slips it out to look at it and behind it is
a picture of his mother as she used to look. Lee is shocked by the
realization that Hank loved his mother.

He goes to his own room, painfully aware of the light coming
from the hole in the wall. He is lying on his bed when Viv comes
to him.

*They are making love when that beam of light cuts off.*

End of Part one<br/>after the second week

Part two would start with Hank. Pick up his narrative when he
leaves the bar. Describe the trip home and the swimming of the
river. *He can't bust right in on them, just because he has just explained his ideas to Lee—but he can't resist looking through the
hole—much much moonlight prior to this on the swim across
especially.* Moonlight so he can see Viv and Lee.

Next day Sunday—a good time for the church scene. Lee goes
with Joe Ben to be out of the house, and away from the discom-

fort. He awakes that morning alone. Viv had left without waking him. He tries to figure what to do. He is scared it might move to a fist fight with Hank—but then he knows he would get her.

He realizes he is in the best position.

*          *          *

"You want to watch the end of one of those branches don't swing around and swat you one."

Wouldn't touch a cigarette from the moment he lit it until it had burned down to his lips and he picked it out and threw it into the mud—a habit picked up smoking while working with wet gloves.

Loader trembling and shuddering under the weight. Drum singing, frenzied motor. Big ice tongs ripping into the juicy bark of logs. Land stroked by great ruts as if a huge snake had crawled through the mud.

Scars in small trees cut by cables—seeming to bleed as the cambium oxidizes bright red.
cold mud clubs of feet . . . clubs of feet registering the blow of striking earth only by the jar in the knees.

Cat dozing logs into a stack
Making a log out of a pile of slashings
Rich live smell of crushed wood
beads of pitch like jewels like grave flowers on stumps of yester-day's trees.

take the shade off the ground
outraged roar of the cat motor
Dutchman
The meadow, washed pale and yellow-green by the months of winter rain, shined like a field of gold under the spring sun.

*          *          *

So the prose has to have the impact of a poem or a painting
that conveys more than is exporable in *this language.*

> I look about me . . . .
> My mind switches into Lee's mind
> My eyes become his eyes
> like the eye dialate with drugs
> and objects are charged with
> his significance:

*Pressed between walls, like a flower, sear and yellow, being
pressed out of its three dimensional world by a book.*
Stumps like tombstones.
LEE      LEE           LEE        LEE       LEE       LEE
LEE      LEE

not just metophors . . . . . . . . . whatelse?

# Lee's
## Hang-up ... ?

His mother's suicide -

He blames himself.
He blames Hank for making to high a mark for him to measure up to.
He blames her for killing herself and god.

Death which is inevitable - so, if so, and if life is not good -) - why put it off?

Hank
Who he feels he must destroy to make it

## So

When death is inevitable, and the absolute finish, + life is all we have — —
    one hand dealt, one hand of cards being dealt -- seven card stud, no draw...
    and, if by the time half your cards are dealt

69

A burning candle in the window
a pair of hands over a book
to do do do—da da da
   a *thing somewhere* in another *thing*

People are gonna *die—not just me*, but also other people—
this is where the french leave off. Xistance is okay for one alone,
*but it doesn't help Moma and daddy or Chuck or Faye—each of
those words, when touched with death, rip a sound like a bell in
my head I can't hardly stand*
Lee has come this far; I have a notion I –– and Hank –– have
gone farther. Let's examine it this way; as already solved and
work backwards to this point.
*Hank wasn't given God to lose.* He's been at it without him
longer. It has grown on him ever since he was a baby; the super-
natural steadily became natural — he was given no other, no
Jesus or god or Holy ghost—only old Henry's whoppers. It came
gradual and wasn't jerked from under his feet like a rug. He was
close to death.
*Keep strong and·you keep something.*
Nothing is *some* thing even if you are there in it.
Maybe death is a new and completely undiscernible concept.
Maybe what you do in this life does influence what happens to you
after death. *Maybe those that don't believe die, not as punishment
but just as fact.*
That child's question "What's it like to be dead?" may not be
so silly. If you can *conceive* of what it's like to be dead you can
begin to adapt to it. A glimpse of hell could be adjusted to, once
accepted.
*Lets say this; death is not like being alive. How then can we
conceive it. It is impossible to conceive of myself being a rock,
but it is possible to be a rock.* It is impossible to conceive of myself being a micro-organism, but it is possible to be composed of
them. It's impossible to conceive of myself as sulfur or nitrogen,

70

but it is possible to be made up of these elements . . . . . . the same elements that are in the stone.

*The stone will not rise up and move. It has no life. It has no choice. I have.*

All is surrounded by mystery. If you look at it long enough it becomes mysterious and intangible.

*The same object that is death to Lee is Life to Hank. How? They argue about a gun. Lee says it's death; Hank says no, picks it up, hefts it, puts it to his shoulder and feels the stock to his cheek and says no it's got a lot of life to it.*

Lee says the only life is in your touch, your sight and smell. An argument follows.

No, more'n that. If they were broken apart, I wouldn't get this feeling.

———They would give you your feeling if you had broken them. It is the memory of what you have done with the gun.

—some, sure; what aint charged with memory; but it's more. I got a feeling, this feeling, the first time I went in the store and picked up that rifle.

—Conditioned reflex—you'd been taught how to feel about rifles.

—No. I picked up others—it was this here gun. Others were different—heavier, lighter, darker in stock—different.

—Are you certain of this feeling? Or are you using it to prove an example when it's not itself proved?

—Let me think———*I reside in me—I take refuge in myself against an onslaught of killers all the time.* When you give you've got to give dear *because it's like dropping brain cells in the beggar's cup—you can't earn them back. When I give somebody a minute of my time it's not like giving him my life savings. Think of it like (for some reason I picture a roll of ticket stubs) you tear one off every minute and give it to somebody.*

Faye has most of my stubs, next to myself. The stubs are used at the same rate no matter if you get them or keep them or don't use them as admission into that minute of life.

When you give to someone you love you double your stubs— she gets one & you keep one. When you give to someone you don't wish to give to that ticket is gone.

This is an argument for Xist again, but I want to be *beyond* Xist, using it.

How?

I must tap senses — unknown senses only suspected, only dreamed of. . . . I must explore all the other world of me. I *sense* the answer is somewhere in there. *Sense* is the key I must use to unlock itself—like a Chinese puzzle box.

*          *          *

Let's consider Hank for a while. How can we make him a truely great and significant character? Let's just look at him a while.

*He listens. He can be seen hunkered on his haunches around tables of his friends, picking at the floorboard with the point of his knife. He thinks things over, but he hasn't lost faith in his instinct yet. He still trusts senses that other men, more sophisticated men, don't recognize.*
But that isn't what makes him great.
He is great because he is *Man the Winner*.

The awareness of life caused by death:

Lee is to some extent the cause of his mother's death. She has always been a weak, draining force, and he finally leaves her to go live with the other girl. His leaving is too much for her. She kills herself. Not in outright suicide, but he knows she did it. She has been a hypochondriac, faking illness until she acquired one that was real. Diabetes would work. He has taken care of her with it before. This time he isn't around when she goes into shock and she dies.
*Instead of feeling guilty, as she would have wanted, he is struck with the fact of his own existence and with that fact, the inevitability that it must end.*
*This is paralleled somewhat by Hank being partly responsible for the uncle's death (or cousin's) Hank is struck with his own life and the futility of it.*
for the first time; he realizes what his not believing in god means.

He has been defeated. His wife would leave him for another man. The Union will take over. The river, year after year will cut away more of the land and carry it to the sea. The sea will win. Meaninglessness, nothingness will win. Over him as well as me, if he doesn't do something.

What can he do?

I see my novel and my lead character now. A winner, a strong man who hates losing being backed, backed, backed into corners — by the water, by losing (the younger brother) by a greater amorphous the Union. Until he is on the brink and he has the great notion to dynamite the cliff, flood the whole thing. And doesn't. Why?

Why? Because he knows to stop fighting is to start dying. And he doesn't accept death. Not the creeping death of religion or the philosophic death of Zen. He believes --- that live can be he --- and can be more than it has been. And that somebody has to fight back the river and the sea if it, love, is ever going to have the chance, in his time or his child's.

Maybe fighting is winning, he realizes. He looks back at his victories and sees they were nothing permanate as he supposed at the time ('he holds athletic records that become defeated). Maybe fighting

is the only winning. He thinks and can't really [think?]
anyone ever losing while they are still fighting.
(He just fights this way -- you can't keep him down.)
Maybe he can do no more; win no more than
fight all his life for the things and the life he
wants.

And when death? This stops him a moment.
Here's something you can't lick. But death
is only death because it is nothingness. He thinks of
his missing fingers and how they rotted in the
jaw no matter how hard he tried to save them. Death
got them, but not him. NOT ME. The
Me, he thinks? Death has already taken so and
so and his body is still alive. But he gave in to
it. But just because Time rots my body and
the water washes over my bones, is that death until
I, ME accept? Concious, Unconcious, moving
still, air or earth, can death get ME if I don't
let it? It can take all my fingers. And my
arms and my body. But me. My Identity.
My individuality? ME? ME?

How can it as long as I remain me. People
flock to churches to seek company, hope in numbers.
But loneliness will triumph if it fights - for me one
for those I love. Because the ME can be made larger
by love. Why?

74

*Outside Hank can hear the current hissing against the pilings.
Keep old Henry thumping and roaring about.*

Joe Ben goes to church. Returns to say the town is growing
restless with the strike. Talk of Faith. *He tells Brower's story of
Jesus coming in the dream. Setting Joe Ben up for death. (new
son, the whole bit)* Lee is quite fond of Joe.

A week. Work, work, work. Trying to beat the winter that has
held off so nice—*In town there is a rumor that the Stamper mill
is selling to the big company.* The strike gets more tense. Soon
winter will set in and there won't be work anyway.

*Maybe Viv goes into town and hears all this. Maybe she doesn't
know the Stampers are prolonging the strike by filling the big
company's contracts. When she finds out it could be a scene with
Hank, a real hassle. Hank considering her proposition, until old
Henry points out that they are in this business to make money. It's
a fight.*

A fight at home, too. Hank and old Henry were the only ones
aware that this was what was going on. A see-saw battle. Old Henry finally has his big scene. He says Lee's in a fight, they all are.
With the goddamned union. Just who do you think the Union is.
Mr. Grey suit? No. It's those people in town that want somebody
to give them security. It's all relative. *If America gets into a war
with Russia, I'm on America's side. If we get invaded from mars
I'll fight with Russia* to put 'em down. If Oregon gets in a fight
with California, I'm on Oregon's side. Figure it on down. If it's
the Stampers against the town, I'm with the Stampers, and if it's
me against the Stampers, I'm with me! You want to know which
side I fight for? The side I'm on. You want to know which side is
the best? The one that wins.

This big hassle shows Hank where he stands. *It is the Stampers
against the town. He's against the Union. Why? Because he's
against being told what to do simply because the scared people
form the majority. The meek shall inherit the earth?* That's just
because there's more of them. Just like the fly would take over if

we let it. *Just like the berryvines would cover the whole town, just like the river would take over the house. Well, if the meek take over this show, they're gonna have to show some spunk doing it.*

*Be hard! Don't let the bastards hook you with sympathy.*

End of a section. A clear cut challenge to the town. Hank's stand on Hardness, toughness. And all the while Lee is taking away his woman with weakness.

Why is Hank so opposed to the union? He pays his men the same as the Union, some of them more. Because it is like the river.

## THE RIVER

When Hank talks to some of the loggers in town he finds they were forced into joining. And they lost something when they did. They have security, money, benefits, a better life . . . but they are somehow out of contact. *These are minor characters to get to know. Old motorcycle buddies of Hanks, slowed down, grown fat, changed. They gave up. They took the easy route. They tried to buck the union for a while (didn't want no fat ass in Portland telling me when and where to work) but pressure becomes too great.*

The pressure of the meek, striving to inherit the earth. These are the men that help beat Hank up. Hank tells them one day when a kid is born they'll just hook a tube to him and ipe him food.

He admits the union has done good. It was men fighting for more, for something else. It isn't any longer. *More has come to be fringe benefits, something else is a better contract.*

But that pressure is there, that steady, smooth pressure of the river. *Hank remembers swimming with the current floating, being swept to sea, the lulling, sleepy rocking feeling of lying on a tube and floating down to Waconda. Falling asleep and almost being washed to sea. That is what has happened to the lives of these two old buddies of his. They have given up, they are just floating to the sea, to death. Because it is easier to die than to live; it always has been.*

You don't live just because your heart pumps blood and your cells feed off of it, no more than you die if this process is squelched. You have to fight for life and freedom and individuality and then fight to keep it.

Hank's lost fingers. Lee asks what about the nerve ends in those fingers that are gone. Aren't you the less for losing them? Can you enjoy the sensation of touch. Hank reaches out with his maimed hand and ties his shoe lace. He says you fight with what you got, not grieve over what you've lost. Old Henry hasn't tasted anything for years, can barely hear, and at the rate he's going will probably be blind before he dies. But he still has things going. The human isn't some kind of complex instrument for receiving stumuli—it is a *will*, a *will*.

*        *        *

### *The story—figure out later what it means*

Pinocchio—the composition of his story. He's born—he receives the rules, breaks them twice but squeaks through at the last. Good composition.

Hank's story. The strong, dauntless man faced with ever in-creasing—pressures all trying to make him give up.

*Try to make Hank give up* is the cry.

We have to establish many reasons for people wanting to make him surrender. One reason: pull down the man on top. This is what Lee did with god. God-Hank-Father these enormous giants, these unbeatable—all sort of one. Lee's bent is to be frightened by them all, to want to drag them from the heavens.

*There should be a scene* establishing this. Hank and Lee's big hassle. *Big argument. Lee has cut down old Henry. Yeah. Maybe told him about Hank and Myra. This means have old Henry not letting* himself be aware of the affair that went on. Change that scene at the first, coming across the water.

So Lee lays the truth on 'Big Daddy'. Old Henry's pride is hurt. *Make him proud of his attraction to women. Make him gloat about taking the young girl away from the New York Society circle.* When Myra leaves make it the *Boy Yes!* Lee's been asking for a long time to leave, but she doesn't consent until Hank is leaving. Old Henry won't make the connection. He blames the boy who has professed a number of times a desire to go to the city, to go back East.

Henry blames Lee for Myra's departure. Not Myra. No. She still loved him. He is vain about this. Viv digs this old vanity and feeds it. Henry (Groupo Kesey) goes to the dance in Waconda. He delights in telling about the way he won that young woman away from the city and kept her twelve years when every one predicted the marriage would last six months at the most.

*This is part of old Henry's courage.*

So . . . Lee chops it down. He tells, in a very cruel way. *Reason?* not cruelty, just pulling down god again

(And at this point old Henry begins his dying; Hank sees that) So . . . Lee chops down old Henry . . Hank lights into Lee. In the presence of Viv tells him he is a weakling and a small man. Tells him he pulled God out of the sky because God was bigger. Not because logic made it necessary. They have had discussions about God. Hank doesn't believe and never has. And—Hank also says he's onto Lee and Lee's reason for returning home. *"You want to drag me down too. Hell, that's nothing new. So does everybody. Ever since I was the bully of the block."*

Then . . . . . . Viv sides with Lee and more pressure on Hank.

---

*But,* back to the *story* and the *plot* that tells the story, and the *technique* that moves the plot.

---

After Lee's home. One day in the woods. Need this first. On the way there meet people and see the pressure. The town has learned that the Stamper mill is providing lumber to the big companies out on strike. *No* not yet. Give Hank a day of popularity in the Waconda bar.

The pressures haven't quite started yet. How to demonstrate their oncoming? Maybe a marker on one of the river pilings. Maybe notice it in every section, see it a little higher. Been a good year, a good summer except for old Henry and Hank is on top.

Drake has lost the papers, yellow papers, that prove Hank is selling to other mills and has to return to Portland for a new set. These he'll present at the local Union meeting next week.

But—that first day. Have PV slip into Lee's mind? And Lee's motivation is still muddy, weak—even to himself. A good time for him to question it? Why has he returned? The question is on Hank's mind too. *Put it there earlier also* in that first passage of Hank's.

On up the slopes. Cuss the donkey. Meet some of the men. Learn the job of choker setting. Watch Hank enjoy the work. Beautiful day. Damn good day, Hank thinks, feeling great. Have him really on top of it. The better he feels the further we can drop him.

Whose PV? Don't know yet.

Lunch. See Viv's lunch. Talk about meeting Viv. Get around to the question, Why did you come back, bub? Why did you come up to these woods?

*Lee answers with a question, asking Hank why he keeps on.* Hank describes his feelings about topping a tree, gets carried away and goes into the description. He loves Lee and wants him to experience the same thing.

He ends the talk really feeling good way *up* ending for section.

Then to Lee at home that night (Hank might have ended the description telling about topping a tree, saying that it makes him feel like a king like there's nothing than can whip him that he feels sometimes down, sometimes scared by the pressures, but up there he knows he doesn't have a weak point at all).

Then cut to Lee watching Viv through the hole in the wall. There, as far as Lee is concerned; is Hank's Achilles heel.

*As far as Lee is concerned*—this means the piece should be in Lee's P.V. so he can just report; a shaded report.

---

## NEXT:

Me— the Big Story Teller—picking up, tying ends together, moving along with the spinning of my tale. About Drake having to return to Portland. About the feeling in town. About Joe Ben and his kid. About the Real Estate man. Making it obvious *I* know that Hank is *up there*, but in for trouble and I'm getting around to it just as fast as I can. I can throw in pertinent bits and pieces, smatterings of dialogue and action—all pertaining to the *Make It Tough on Hank* theme that I'm developing.

What does this remind me of? The narrator on Elliot Ness: "as so and so were doing *this* such-and such was on his way into town to do this . . . "

So, I say, when Hank and Lee and Joe Ben go into town Saturday night the townspeople were still on good terms with them (because Drake hadn't returned).

There's been some rain in the higher hills.

The river has started to rise.

\*　　　　　\*　　　　　\*

Notes from the middle of a scene:

With nothing ahead but unknown territory and what's gone behind pretty murky itself . . halting, with a scene half over, after a half a joint and other such digressions, to take stock of where I stand and what the land looks like from here.

I didn't know what was supposed to happen, exactly.

And, even more important, I didn't know to whom it was supposed to happen to . . .

(and notes in the middle of Notes In the Middle of: I am too influenced by the future reader when I type, for even when I'm writing only for myself I have an eye out for the other guy who will read it. Not so as much with handwriting because it seems more like writing a diary)

To get back:

What is to happen to whom?

Secretly, to the reader.

But openly, to Lee

\*　　　　　\*　　　　　\*

There is the sound of work—in the woods, in the distant woods, like the sound of insects in the walls.

House, unsided yet—vertical—corners, two-by-four white pine stripes, even and regular—horizoned ceiling beams, floor beams, window sills, door sills—and diagonal—room, x-ing reinforce-ments, criss-crossing, up and down, back and forth crosspatch skeleton against the moon, wood warping for lack of paint, the thing that's wood be a house stark and baffled, a home for dead leaves and the wind.

My book is trying maybe too goddamn much, trying to encom-pass a man, a family, a town, a country, and a time—all at once, simultaneously, and work them into a story, and have the story say something important. Awful much, Awful much.

Woman in colored glasses with white rims.

Mexican looking for work, opening sunflower seeds with his thumbnails, squinting against the sun reflected white hot from new pine planks as he approaches the men working.

\*         \*         \*

Lee has trapped himself worse than ever because he loves Viv, but has forced Hank into fighting to keep her so when Hank punches him he can't understand it at all—and doesn't until much later. (this is a scene when Lee comes to him to tell off Hank's re-versed decision)

So let's assume all that.

Now.

I'm going to start back through this way.

Read it with as little rewriting as I can get by with, making notes to myself.

Decide on arrangement and order.

Get the voices true.

Shape up the conflicts.

Begin to think of it as a whole.

much more interesting because the interest is in the discovery so I can't possibly (Hagen) push too much.

The cells know. Keep your ear up tight against the cells, like against a worn rail in the sun listening for the train.

An image images should but with a flash—solid—never some-thing for the reader to delve at the symbols—fast—click—so to write a scene what about we block in from imagery high points

81

first? Let's just see—Leaving the house. Henry and Lee and Viv dropping back to give the old man an easier time images you don't write?

Perhaps the sustained drive can only be accomplished *as* it is accomplished, which means for me, at least here *now*, in this junction of space time high, that I must keep the pen moving across the paper and just see where it comes, like firing at random to keep from falling asleep, like putting paint on a canvas and discovering—and *discovering* is the word—moving with each idea, each image, on into the next—so we create a feeling by connecting a series of images that in my mind gave me that feeling so we have the job of the lawn sprinklers.

I have all these things going at once, is one of the troubles and I can't ever get situated properly to administer to each the attention it deserves, so again, keep pushing the pen forward to see where it lands.

Like for one thing I get a feeling about a thing all in a flash, general like the feeling I had when I found Larry had come out back to the very woman I was trying to keep out of his sight. I had this flash of feeling that this would be a good thing to pursue but didn't fool with it because I had sped on to something else.

Moths: soft, puffy all over the table filling the soft white light of my desk lamp with their fluttering.

the sound of last night's rain leaving the eaves, dripping from the leaves.

\*            \*            \*

Hunting scene—after supper going up to the top of the hill overlooking the house. That's as far as the old man can go, Henry, Viv and Lee stay. Lee and Viv begin talking guardedly so as not to let old Henry know what they are about. Eventually he falls asleep but they keep the symbolic talk going.

This is when the dog somes back with the snake hung in her.

Henry listening to hands while they talk,

As Listener listens to Boney tell the Stamper story we have
(1)  Billy's thoughts
(2)  The Juke
(3)  Viv & Lee's conversation


I think perhaps from this point in the book on it may be best to *assume* what happens, outline it sketchily perhaps, but compose no more.

For these reasons:

I fear I may already have more going than I can gracefully handle and as I write more I get more. I think it time to go to work on what I have instead of adding more.

So.

From here on out let us tentatively say that this is what is going to happen:

Hank sees the town needs his stubbornness. (Football team loses etc.) is pressured into delivering load. Therefore loses Viv to Lee. When Viv goes to town to tell the two events.

"Yes . . No!" No, there aint a comparison.

Writer becomes irritated. "All right didn't this man migrate here at a certain point in your life—Yes—Okay. That happens say we number it by years that happens year 8 in your life. In year 10 or it could be page numbers couldn't it?" slyly, confident.

No. Cause I didn't think nothing about it till year 60.

Should I pick up this old man as a narrator? A voice in parenthesis? Italics?

What about this: could I have 3 things going at once and have them occasionally interact like History, family meeting Lee driving out after Joe's Telegram. Click right there end of section?

Splicing? Quick glimpse of scenes to come. Quick images.

We're going along when a line triggers an image in the future. The image occurs some way. Finally the scene going and the scene sneaking in mesh and the scene sneaking in takes over.

Or like scenes in a morning dissolving into one another as scene gaining reaches its end we have already slipped in exposition for scene to come. Like background noise coming in over scene or background noise incongrous to *what is happening* at the moment before your eyes, but fitting with what is to happen. (train whistle out to see—cut to train bearing down.)

I have how many distinguishing forms to occur at once?
3rd person-past
1st person past
3rd person-present
1st person-present
2nd person? (old man talking to writer?)
Parenthesis
Italics


dog good for bear hunt

two paragraphs that are nice but don't quite work. Haven't established technique clearly yet.

Old man reporter questions should explain the technique as he explains that he can't just know the Stampers, or the area, or the job but has got to know it from all angles of time from everybody's angle every place . . . that's the only way to understand what went on. My story is just my story of what happened, not the whole story. To get the whole story you got to do better and look at it through Les Libbon's eyes, or mine, or anybody's--you got to get clean around it like a stafish belly.

But how do I do this, how do I get the reader to surround a story when the words can only come out one at a time.

Okay, he could say it started so many days ago—to the eye. That's when, say, it actually got all its parts together and moving. I could tell you that. But happening right alongside are things in 1930, 1920, clear back to 1800. Something like this don't start at one place and move along like the alphabet. It ain't that way. (the writer is trying to take notes) Writer doesn't understand. Old guys get agitated. For instance, Ben 1907 Jonas Stamper comes out here. Some time 1960 Lee comes out from New York.
"I am a man more sinned against than sinning," says poor old Lear.

Buddy, aren't we all. It's a battle from the word go. If the water tank ain't dry its a goddamm flood. If you ain't hung up because you're hungry you're hung up because you've feasted. And the gun is on you every breathing day.

Things to add whenever possible

    A cigar is just a cigar but a good woman is a fuck.
Tomorrow's nothings.
Skagit yarder or loader, like a prehistoric monster.
furls of blue smoke at noon, rising from solitary launches.
Death is the color of rust.
Greyish red, grey over red, red under grey.
Unloading sacks of dried blood from a box car.
Men so tiny alongside the trees.
It isn't life against death, it's man against death rotted snags like
skeletons.

and humble

~~in his stomach.~~ Some nights, after ~~xx~~ standing head-bowed before the
~~dxx~~ drunken spray of one of his patrons, he would ~~stand~~ have to consider for a half an
hour ~~our~~ or more at this end of the bar, smiling, with one hand lightly
on the bartop like something onborn, before the throbbing lights could
massage away the ~~pain of the bruises and soothe the little screaming~~ outrage
~~things he called his "furies".~~ During these periods he seemed quite undaged; He greated each new arrival with his
usual formal manner; he fiddled with ~~kix~~ the long keychain that lpoped
across ~~xix~~ the round bulge of his apron; he called out the hour when asked..②
~~Outwardly, when he stationed~~ stood ~~at this end of the bar, nothing was~~ waiting for a new ~~man cut to move~~
~~different, except the pulsing hues~~ ①but wearing ~~of his face that~~ which shifted ~~from green~~
~~to red to deep violet with the ax pulsing of the lights.~~

"Billy, you little octopus, could you come down here an' pour some
clear look Gilbert's Gin
of that stuff out of that ~~Johnny Walker~~ bottle into this glass of mine?
There's a good boy..."

~~Was~~ fifty cents please, Mr. Evenwrite..."

"Fifty **cents**? You askin' money for this? Billy, I wasn't aimin'
with it "
to drink it; I was goin' into the head and give myself a shampoo, ~~it~~ — "

The men laugh, turning from their serious, down-to-business talk,
eyelid
welcoming the comic relief. Billy flutters his ~~eyes, xxxx~~ looking
he might faint dead away with the weight of gin
~~as though~~ he might burst into tears, The men slap a fifty cent piece
down onto the bar ~~xxxkxxxgx~~ like ~~x~~ it was a bug to be squashed③.. they laugh,
this the laughter and an
But ~~tonight~~, inspite of ~~the xxxxxxxxxx and xxxxxxx~~ collection an
uncommon ~~lot~~ of bruising insults, Billy spent very little time recuperating
under the healing flood of his lights. He was too busy, for one thing.
of the trips to the Stampers
With the spreading of ~~Johnny Draeger's~~ story, the bar had become more and
Jonathan Draeger had suggested to Evenwrite that②
more crowded. Evenwrite had been on the telephone almost from the moment
they returned ~~from their trip~~ (upriver) ~~to the Stampers, calling to tell~~ tell
pass the call on
the boys what had happened, and ~~telling~~ them to ~~call.~~ There had been a
reminding

Present tense
Present tense

① from the mortification of it

② he seemed quite the same as he always did, ~~tremoulous,~~ ~~remote, preoccupied~~ ... and those who might have studied him standing there would have attributed the hues of red and orange and magenta shifting over his face to nothing more than the pulsing neons.

③ You live too long with the dogs you forget that ~~lions share the same earth, breath the same~~ ~~for ours~~, ~~eat the same food~~. You must ~~not~~ forget.

④ it might not be a bad idea to call a few of the members and inform them of the outcome and

There had been a     neon arch

steady parade through the ~~big glass door~~ for the last hour as the men

poured in--loggers, truckers, sawyers, xxxx the two government-hired

scalers out-of-work ~~them~~selves until the strike ended, even the fisher-

men brought from their warm, rocking cabins by the sound of so many cars

driving up main on a weeknight. ~~Billy knew there was nothing like~~

~~some bad news, nothing like~~ a good flood or war scare or ~~such, to get men~~

~~together for serious drinking.~~ He remembered ~~pulling twice the liqua~~

~~volume on the Sunday night after Pearl Harbor as~~ he'd moved on VE day

~~and VJ~~ shuffed back and forth along the smooth bar

as soundless and graceful as a sea creature, deftly filling jiggers
          in the face of constant jibes and cuts
and drawing beers and was far too busy to afford himself the luxery of

pouting under his lamps. For one thing.

   And, for another, didn't need the balm of his lights xx ~~nearly as~~

~~much as usual~~; he was soothed by the muted pitch of worry, of troubled
                    blending                              with
voices and angry words, ~~that rose~~ xxxxxxxxx from each table xxx the

rising smoke of hundreds x of cigarettes ~~and congealed heavy and blue~~

~~over the room.~~

   At all the tables the conversation x followed essentially the

same lines, starting with they'd never thought it of Hank Stamper--

old Henry, maybe, but Hank's always been a pretty good ol' boy, on to

"What the devel? you can't expect to get a peach off'n a thorn-apple

bush, can you? Just Because Hank aint always all the time juiced out

tellin' about how you got to have a armor-plated hide to make a go of

this business, like the old man all the time is, don't mean he aint

blood of blood and flesh of flesh! And eventually on to There's no

two ways about it that I can see: Hank Stamper's showed where he stands

and he's just got to be showed the x error of his ways.

   "And I for one say," ~~Evenwrite~~ shouted, jumping to his feet and

# And when one of these ~~frightfully drinking days~~ ~~days for~~ drink-and-deepen days occurred Billy felt himself invulnerable to the clutching tongues. and hung in the air.

⑤ ~~Perhaps~~ "Billy, I tell you, " they called, and indicated the drink, the bill, ~~the~~ perhaps the fickle juke box; " I tell you something wrong here. Rose blending and hung congealed & flue over the room. Billy breathed deep & didn't need the resuscitation of neon

sweeping the room with gin-bright eyes, "say we go right back out there

and put Mister Hank Stamper straight!"

There was a low growl of approval, but the bar was too warm and

bright and the night outside too cold and wet, and Johnny Drager, sitting

sober and still chilled from his boat ride, knew these men better than

to imagine imagine them as a mob. He waited and kax studied the facets

of colored light in the shot glass he twisted in his fingers, while

Evenwrite banged about the tables cursing and taunting the men, redfaced

with gin and

"Whadya say! Whadya say! Right on out there and we'll--" he blinked,

concentrating fiercly "...and we'll just the whole bunch of us we'll--"

"Swim across the river like a pack of beavers?" The heads turned

from Evenwrite to Drager. "Stand on the bank and throw rocks?"

Evenwrite snatched up his empty glass and glared at it as though

though the calm, deep voice was issuing from it's mouth.

"Use your head, Floyd. running out to that house like a bunch of fools out of a

cowboy movie even if we could find a legal way because

"Legal! " Evenwrite shouted at the glass. "What

the shit's legal got to do?"

"...because," Drager went on, across the

river. even if we did get across we couldn't get passed that cordant

of wolves they surround the place with.

The men laughed uncertainly, puzzled by the calm tact of this man

who had been so eager at the grange hall just a night ago to whip them

into action. They waited, watching him glass. Evenwrite spun

around to the bar, by

demanding a free glass on account of damnit for all the gin he'd

90

① But when he didn't go on the crowd turned its attention back to Evenwrite, who still stood clutching his empty glass. Someone laughed Evenwrite spun to see who,

Someway this Drager had made him the fool again, though damned if he could see how. He tried to study the tact for a moment, then gave it up and vented his frustration on Billy.

② Billy wasn't worried that he might lose any sales. As warded up as they were he knew better than worrying them a mob. He peeked up through his lashes and saw that Jonathan Draeger, sitting near the electric heater to let the big fans drive out the chill, was no more worried about being trampled in a riot than he was.

③ "So whateveryou say we get with it."
Most of them said yeah but none of them moved.

④ "in the first place we couldn't get across the river as a group. Unless you think Mr. Stamper would ferry us across two or three at a time. I've never met the man," he smiled about at the room, "but from all I've heard I don't think I'd care to go across as an emissary and request that he bring enough of us across to make up a mob. Of course, Floyd, you may be so inclined. I hear you're more skilled at this sort of thing than I am."

91

xxxx bought there tonight if it', been real stuff he'd be drunk on his
ear, now aint that so? Without comment, Billy refilled the glass.
Evenwrite drank it with a gulp, not even closing his eyes. "Pigeon
Piss," he xxixxx decided and spit in the direction of the spitoon. There
was a little wave of laughterx, still uncertain, xx the men xxxxxxx xxxx
xxxxxxxx xxxixxlocalxpresidentxandxtheirxRepresenxitixxx looked back and
their local president to their representative, xxxxx xxxxxx
forth from/EvenwritexxkexDrager. Drager seemed unaware of the silence
that had risen up after his words, and peered through his twisting glass
xxxx xxxxxxxxxxxx xxxxx. Evenwrite felt himself still on the spot somehow,
and finally xxxxxxxx broke the quiet by xxxxxxxxx throwing the glass
after his spit at the x brass pot wired to the corner of the bar and
shouting "Pigeon Piss," again. "That aint gin, that's pure hunred fifty
proof pigeon piss." He turned, toward Drager, leaning slightly, with his
eyes very bright. "Axxx Okay Drager since your so fuckin' smart lets
here what you say we should do. You called this walkout the first place.
Aint that so? Since your so smart okay let's xxxxxxxxxxxxxxx hear xxx
what you're gonna do to get us outta this mess. I'm jus' a dumbass sawyer!
                    dumbasses
I x mean, nobody pays us/to think. Since your so fxxxxx smart—"
Drager xxx the glass down on the fermica table top, xxxxx xxxxxxx xxx
xxxxxxx xlixkr "If you'll just sit down and take it easy, Floyd/xxx xxx xxx—"
From behind his bar Billy watched and marvelled at the man's smooth,
controled power
" He HexDon't you Floyd xxxx me, Drager. Let's xx xkay lets wake up and
die right. Goddamnit; you know and I know what we gotto do. Maybe we
xx beat our gums here the rest the night but we know! An' me hollering
to go out there after Stamper was a dumbass thing, sure. But not no
more dumbass than you suckin' us into this strike none of us wanted!"
"None of you wanted? You was all xxxxx starving to death to hear
you tell it a month or so back last August.

                              92

① a muffled yet resonant click, sounding at once distant
and very near like a click heard underwater

② , his eyes patient and his smile pleasant and
affable.

Late August

"~~A month or so back~~ you told us we'd settle without a walkout!"

"One
To get it out

^You scared ~~of a little fight~~, Floyd? Scared you might miss a

couple of paychecks?"
so softly that it was difficult tell if the voice came from hi

Drager still spoke ~~softly, smiling; but~~ Evenwrite's voice ~~got~~
or not.
overpower
grew louder ~~as though he hoped~~ to ~~drown xxxx~~ the silence that Drager had

brought down on the room. "N~~o~~ I ain'~~t~~ scared to miss a couple of paychecks!
quitted
I done it before~~,~~ ^ll of us have. We've struck before and we've ~~struck it~~
out. And will do it again, won't we boys?
A~~i~~nt that so? A~~i~~nt it?" He looked about at the men, nodding. ~~Some of~~
What was what the xxness is askiy
the men nodded with him, watching Drager. ~~"And well xxxxx strike again~~
You're right we will.
get it on  couple  Prayer
~~most like!~~ We aint scared to miss a paycheck ~~,~~ but we aint scared to
dead whipped
back off when we're ~~dxxxxxxxxxxg~~, neither!"

"Floyd, if you'll--"
whipped comin' for goin'
"A~~n~~d we are whipped! ~~Let's, let's wake up an die right!~~" He stopped

speaking to Drager and turned toward the men again. "~~Right,~~ I been wantin'

to cash it ~~in~~ a long time now~~,~~. It was the wrong time of year to walk out;
hell, middle of winter ...
we all knew that,^ But Drager figured if he could just swing this one he

was on his way to him a big spot, so he got us--"

"Floyd..."
Drager, if you're so budgin' smart..."
Check "~~Boys, we got obligation & we got~~"
light  touch  stored, would ...Billy as he
Again ~~came~~ that ~~xxx shard~~, restrained ~~click~~ of the glass against the
do light as a hammer cocking.
table~~,~~^ The heads swung back to Drager. From behind his bar Billy ~~stored~~ ~~watched~~
Johnny Drager.
~~and~~ marvelled at the man's power~~x~~ and timing...No idiot him, he knows how
As soon as he
to wait. ~~As drager~~ started speaking ~~the men seemed to~~ ~~xxxxally~~ ~~until they~~ idiot draw~~n~~ toward~~s~~

~~him without leaving their places~~, straining ~~inward~~ without motion toward
like metal particals
his soft voice ~~as xxxxxx~~ strain in toward ~~xxxxxxx~~ a magnate...
Orland Stamper
"Floyd...doesn'~~t~~ the ~~foxxxxx~~ foreman from the Stamper mill, live
,
right next door to you?"
don't
... ~~x~~Straining in to him without even moving, ~~Billy thought,~~ it ~~don't~~,

make any difference what he says. Because he's a force, a force, and

94

\*      \*      \*

After two successful novels and ten times two successful fantasies I find myself wondering "What to prove next? I've shown the buggers I can write, then shown them I can repeat & better the first showing, now what do I prove?"

The answer seems to be "prove nothing."

"A clever challenge, Chaps, and one, I confess, that stirs the fight in me. Now _anyone_ can crank out a nice compact comercial, slide it between covers and vend it as literature,

⟨2⟩

but how many are there capable
of advancing absolute proof
of nothing?"

"Not many, no, not so very many."
"Then, by jingo," slapping his thighs
vigorously, "let's do it!"

SLIDE BACK FOR ANSWER

How How How How How

too far

96

The **Seven Prayers by Grandma Whittier** appeared in a slightly different form in **Spit in the Ocean,** issues one and two, a magazine © copyright 1976 by Ken Kesey. All rights are reserved by Ken Kesey.

**Seven Prayers** will be completed in seven issues of **SITO.** The rates for **SITO** are: $2 for single issues, $5 for three, and $10 for all seven. Address: **SITO,** 85829 Ridgeway Rd., Pleasant Hill, Oregon 97401.

Ken Kesey calls **Seven Prayers** "form in transit." The parts of this new novel are subject to change as it grows longer and more complete. The first two sections as they appear here are complete and reflect the most recent form of the form in transit.

# SEVEN PRAYERS

## by Grandma Whittier

### Good Friday

*Dearest Lord Jesus Christ have mercy on this poor confused tormented and just plain scared-silly old soul down on her bony knees in the dark for the first time in Heaven knows how long begging bless me and forgive me but honest to betsy Lord i always figured that for one thing You had enough sparrows to keep Your eye on and that for another You had done answered this old bird her lifetimes share the time after papa and uncle dicker topple and brother took us kids to the turn-of-the-century worlds fair in little rock and i saw the wild man from borneo running around in a cage all ragged black and half naked with hair sticking out a foot making this crazy low and lonesome sound way down in his chest as he chased after a white chicken and finally caught it right where the crowd had pushed me up against the bars so as i couldnt help but see every yellow fang in his slobbery mouth as he bit that chicken neck slick in two then hunkered down there staring directly into my popeyes chewing slobbering*

99

*and would you believe grinning till i could not help myself but to go and throw up all over him which peeved him so he give a howl of awful rage and run his hand out through the bars at me screeching such a rumpus that the sideshow man had to go in the cage with a buggy whip and a stool and drive him back whining in a corner of the filthy old cage but not before i got my bonnet tore off and had been put in such a state that poppa had to leave the other kids with uncle dicker and take me home sick with the shakes so abiding terrible that from that night on through the entire summer i could not be left alone in my dark room without a burning lamp and even then still had practically every nights rest ruint by these horrible nightmares how this black man not a negro but a wild primitive black man that had been trapped and took from his home and family in the jungles of borneo and was therefore already crazed with savage lonesomeness and hate and humiliation was bound and determined to bust out of that puny little sideshow pen and come after me because of the way i had vomited at the loathsome sight of him and one late autumn afternoon sure as shooting i had just walked little emerson t home from playing in our yard because it was getting on dusk and on my way from the whittier place coming back towards topples bottom i saw the cane shaking and something coming through the canebrakes and heard a kind of choked-off baying wheezing and moaning sound so chilling i froze cold in my tracks as it come closed and closer till O Lord there he was that big old ball of black hair and that mouth and that chicken flopping in his hand lumbering out of the cane right at me then you can bet i run run screaming bloody murder right acrost the roadruts through the gorse stickers and in that dim light blundered over the edge of a gully and lit headfirst in a pile of junk farm machinery and scrap-iron that brother had put there to keep the soil from gullying away so fast and laid there on my back in kind of a coma so as i was still awake and could see and hear perfectly well but could not move so much as muscle nor mouth to holler for help while tearing through the gorse and dust and blackberries right on down at me here come this wild black head and Loving Jesus as though i wasnt already scared enough to melt now i saw that he was not only going to get me but i wouldnt even be mercifully passed out so i prayed Lord i prayed in my mind like i never prayed before nor till this instant that if i could just die just happily die and not be mortified alive that on my solemnest oath i*

100

*would never ask another blessed thing so help me Great Almighty God but then i saw it wasnt the wild man from borneo after all it was only the mute half-wit colored boy that lived with the whittiers cropping hands and as was the occasional custom of the coloreds at that time he had stole a legern pullet from the whittiers coop and the sound i had heard was a mix-up of his cleft-pallet moaning the chicken squawking and whittiers old redbone hound bawling after him in a choked-off fashion because mr whittier kept the dog chained to a six-pound cannon ball from his navy days that the dog was towing behind him through the brush and i thought oh me i prayed to die and now i am going to lie here paralyzed and bleed to death or something and not be mortified after all but then that mute boy seen me hurt at the bottom of the gully and tossed the chicken to the hound and climbed down and picked me up and carried me out of the gully and back through the stickers onto the road just in time for my uncle dicker to take one look at me all bloody being toted by a goo-gawing black idiot and knock him down with a cane stalk and beat him nearly to death before his daughter my cousin sara run to get papa who brought me on into pine bluff in the back of his wagon with my head a bloody mess yet still wide-open-eyed in mamas lap and the boy roped behind the wagon gaping and gagging at me in the lanternlight for me to tell them but i couldnt speak no more than he could while all the way uncle dicker and brother and the other men who joined our little procession kept talking about hangings too good for the drooling inbred maniac he oughta be burnt or worse till they carried me on into doctor ogalvies downstairs parlor and undressed me and cleaned me and doctored my wound as best they could with the doctor shaking his head at papa and mama and my sisters crying all the time me seeing the lanterns passing back and forth on the porch and hearing brother and the men talking louder and louder about what they aimed to do to that boy should i not pull through like it looked like i wasnt and then my eyes finally closed and i let out a long last breath and sure enough i died. It was the queerest thing. I sailed right up out of my body while Doctor Ogalvie was saying I'm sorry, Topple; she's gone—sailed right over the town through the night right on up to Heaven where the streets were lit with pure gold and the angels were playing harps and the moth I presume did not corrupt. Heaven. But when I started to go through the gates that were all inlaid pearl precisely like there are supposed to be this huge tall angel with an enormous book says to me Wait a minute, little girl; what's your name? I says Becky Topple and he says Becky Topple? Rebecca Topple? I thought so, Becky; you have been marked by the Blood of the Lamb of God Almighty and you aren't due up here for another good seventy-seven years! The Son of Man Hisself has you down for not less than one entire century of earthly service! You're to be a saint, Rebecca; did you know that? So you got to go on back, honey. I'm sorry . . . And sent me sailing back through the clouds and the stars to Arkansas and Pine Bluff and Doctor Ogalvie's house all fluttering at the parlor windows with torches and kerosene lamps like big angry millers and right down through the roof. I swear it was absolutely the queerest sensation, seeing my body in that room with all my folks and family crying and little Emerson T. struggling with his papa to get to me crying Becky aint dead aint dead cant be dead as I just drifted back into my body like so much smoke being sucked back down a chimney and took a breath opened my eyes and set up and told them that that mute boy had not harmed me. No. Quite the contrary that I'd been fooling around that gully and fell into the scrapiron and he had come along and seen me and saved me, thank the Lord (I had my fingers crossed, I bet, and said another Thank the Lord to myself) and I have never bothered you about another single thing since that, Jesus, as I solemnly promised. What was there for me to ask, actually? I have never doubted that angel with the book. Not from that instant to this have I ever feared mortal danger, nor never thought I would have to, either —leastways until nineteen eighty-five or so rolled around. And I always figured that by then I would be more than tickled to be getting shut of this wore-out carcass and battered old mug anyhow. So I swear to You with God and that tall angel as my witnesses that I am not shivering scared here on my knees like some dried-up old timer miser pinchin life like her last measly pennies. Because I'm not. What I am asking for is I guess a sign of some kind, Lord; not more time. Running out of time simply is not what I'm scared of. What I am afraid of I can't put a name to yet, having just this day encountered it like finding a new-hatched freak of nature, but it is not of dying. Moreover I am not even sure whether my fear is of a real McCoy danger or Not. Is this dirty business I think I perceive really occuring? or has the pure and simple weight of years finally made its crack in my reason like it has in poor Miss Lawn and in loony Mr. Firestone and his communists behind every bush and in so many other tenants at the Towers lots of whom I know are way younger than me—made its cruel crack in my mind so that all these sudden fears these shades and behind-every-bush boogers that seem to have leaked in are nothin more than just another wild black mistake from Borneo this old white hen is making . . . is what I'm wanting to know, Lord Jesus, is the sign I'm praying for*

She raised her face, hearing the log train toot past Nebo Junction. Bringing the week's logging down from Blister Creek. Unless they had changed their schedule sometime since those sleepless nights years ago it meant it was getting near midnight. Good Friday's about to turn, she thought wryly, into what I guess a body might call Bad Saturday. She shook her head; it just didn't feel like Eastertime. Too warm. This was the first time Easter had been late enough in April to have Good Friday fall on her birthday since—she ducked her chin once more to her hands clasped at the neck of her gown—since it must of been the first summer after marrying Emery. That first Oregon holiday. It was hot and peculiar then, too. Maybe it'd cool some yet, bring down the usual shower on the egg hunt. She frowned. She couldn't recall what Fred Paddle's weekend forecast had been on last night's Final Edition, but she knew the valley skies well enough to know there wasn't a Chinaman's chance for cooler weather by Sunday, much less rain. Driving out from Eugene this afternoon she'd noticed a lot of farmers already irrigating. Now, the night air around her was dry as a bone. "Makes me feel about as much like Easter as snow in July would make you feel like the Fourth." She spoke aloud to try to calm her trembling but her own voice sounded so totally unfamiliar that it only added to her anxiety. She clenched her lips and reminded herself again that this was their old cabin, out at their old Nebo place. Then how come everything seemed so hellish unfamiliar as to make her doubt her judgment of recent events? Because it was her first night away from her safe little apartment in so long? No, she decided, shaking her head. No, no, no; that don't account for it. I spent Christmas and New Years at Lena's and was no crazier than usual. Besides, I felt it *before* I left the apartment. The moment my grandson phoned I told him I didn't want to go. I says "Why, boy, tonight the Reverend Dr. W. W. Poll is having an Inspiration Service down in the lobby that I *couldn't miss!*" Ugh, he groans, having accompanied me a time or two and knowing that the Doctor's services are about as inspirational as a mud fence. "He's better than my sleeping prescription," I says, kidding him so's he won't notice and be hurt. So I felt it then. He kept at me, though. He's like his Grandpa that way, when he gets a notion he thinks is for somebody else's good. I carried the phone over to turn down Secret Storm, giving excuses right and left till at length he sighs and says "Okay, the *real reason* is we are all having a surprise birthday party for you." I says, "Honey, I sure do thank you but when you get past eighty a birthday party is about as welcome a surprise as a new wart." He says that I hadn't been out to visit them in close to a year, blame my hide, and he wants me to see how they've fixed the place back up. Like for a grade, I thought; another trait of his Grandpa's. I told him I was sorry but I did not have the faintest inclination to aggravate my back jouncing out to the dadgummed old saltmine even if they'd put in a field of orchids . . . "It was forty years out there put me in this pitiful condition," I tell him, though it isn't really my back, the doctor says, but a gall bladder business aggravated by sitting, especially in a moving car. "Baloney," he says. "Besides, the kids have all baked this fantastic birthday cake and decorated it for Great Grandma's birthday; their dear little hearts will be broken." I tell him to bring them and their dear little hearts both on into my apartment and we'd drink Annie Green Springs, pull taffy and watch the people down in the parking lot. Ugh, he says again. He can't stand the Towers. He maintains that our lovely 20-story ultra-modern apartment building is nothing more than a highrise plastic air-conditioned *tomb*stone where they stick the corpses waiting for graves. Which it is I can't deny but, plastic or no, I make just enough on my Social Security and Natural Gas royalties to pay my way if I take advantage of Poor People's Housing. My *own* way. He don't understand. He's always after me to move back out to the farm with him and Betsy, saying how fine it would be for everybody, especially the kids, to be able to have a bonafide pioneer mother tell them how it was making lard out of ashes and ink out of onions; I explain I'd ruther be a complete and total shutaway than a piece of bric-a-brak. But he don't understand.

"I appreciate the invitation, sugar, but I guess I hadn't better disappoint the Reverend W. W. Poll. Not when he's just a short elevator ride as opposed to a long ordeal in an automobile. So you all bring that cake on over here. It'll do us old geezers good to see some kids besides Charlie Brown." He laughed and told me the cake was too big to move. I says *too big?* and he says that they was having not only my party but a whole day long to-do with music and a service their ownselves and quite a few people expected. A sort of Worship Fair, he called it. "Al-so," he says, in that same way he used to twist me around his finger as the first of the grandkids: ". . . *all*-sooo, The Sounding Brass are going to be here." Grandkids always have your number worse than any of your own kids, and the first is the worst by a mile. "Don't you flim-flam *me*, Bub!" But he says Scout's Honor, Grandma. I says Scout's bull, too; not *thee* Sounding Brass. He says cross his heart; he picked them all up at the bus depot not three hours ago, swallowtails, buckteeth and all, and they have promised to sing a special request for my birthday, even though they don't usually dedicate songs and haven't done it in years," "And I will wager," he says, "you can't guess which one." His words some way more extravagant than's even usual for him. I don't answer. I heard it then. I knew what the song would very likely be, but I was still listening to how funny his voice had sounded in the earpiece. "Too thrilled to take a guess?" Now he *knows* I'm not your swooning bobby-soxer, even over the Brass family. But it wasn't that, exactly. . . "They are going to sing that version of *Were You There* that you used to like so much." I say "You remember *that?* Why, it's been twenty years since I had that Victrola if it's been a day. More like thirty." He said *all*-so as far as the ride went they had a special bus with a full-sized bed in it coming for me at four on the dot: "So don't give me any more of that bad back baloney. This is your day to party!" I realized what it was, too: there was somebody else with him, standing near at the other end of the line while he talked so he was grooming his voice for more than just his granny. Not Betsy, nor Buddy. Somebody else. After we hung up I was in a kind of a dither trying to think who. I started to turn my program back up but it was the ad for denture stickum where that middle-aged ninny is eating peanuts and laughing at his own muleheaded jokes. So I just switched the wretched thing clean off and stood there by the window, looking down at Eugene's growing traffic situation. Zoom zoom zoom a silly bunch of bugs. The Towers is the highest building in all Lane County unless you count that little one-story windowless and doorless cement shack situated on top of Skinner's Butte. Some kind of municipal transmitter shack is I guess what it is. I have no idea what's in it. Radio business I suspect. It was up there just like it stands today the very first time Emerson T. and me rode to the top of the Butte. We drove if I'm not mistaken a spanking brand new 1935 Terraplane Sedan of a maroon hue that Emerson had bought with our alfalfa sales that spring. Eugene wasn't much more than a main street, just some notion stores and a courthouse and Quackenbush's Hardware. Now it sprawls off willy-nilly in all directions as far as a person can see, like some big old monopoly game that got out of hand. Changing faster almost than you can keep up with it. It seems peculiar to me now how that little shack is the only thing I can think of unchanged and I still don't know what's in it. I picked up Emerson T.'s fieldglasses from my sill and took them out of their leather case. They're army glasses but Emery wasn't in the army; when they wouldn't let him be a chaplain he became a consciencious objector. He won the glasses at bingo. I like to use them to watch the passenger trains arrive Monday nights, but there isn't much to watch of a Friday noon. Just that new clover-leaf, smoking around in circles. Oh *why*ever had I let him make me say yes? I could still hear my pulse rushing around his words in my ears. I turned the glasses rear-way-around and looked for a while that way, to try to make my heart slow its pit-a-pat (nope, it hadn't been Betsy or Buddy, nor *none* of his usual bunch that I could think of offhand. . .) when, without so much as a by-your- leave or a kiss-my-foot, there, right at my elbow, sucking one of my taffy-babies and blinking those bloodrare eyes of hers up at me was that dadblessed Miss *Lawn!* "Oh Mrs. *Whit*tier?" Those eyes made me jump like a frog. She puts away as much as a quart of Vin Rose before lunch somedays; she told me so her-self. "You're looking through the *wrong end* again, Mrs. Whit-tier," she says as she shuffles from foot to foot in those gum-rub-ber slippers she wears. In a breath that would take the bristles off a hog. . . "Excuse me, but I heard your *television* go off then when it didn't come *back on I* was worried something might be the matter. . . ?" She wears those things for just that purpose, too: slipping. I know for a fact that as soon as she hears my toilet flush or one of my pill bottles rattle she slips into her bathroom to see if my medicine cabinet is left open; our bathrooms are back-to-back and the razorblade disposal slot on her medicine cabinet lines right up with the razorblade disposal slot on my medicine cabinet and if she don't watch out one of these days I'm going to take a fingernail file and put one of those poor bloodshot eyeballs out of its misery. Not really. We're old acquaintances, actually.

Associates. Old maids and old widows of a feather. I tell her if she must know I turned if off to talk over the telephone. "I *thought* I heard it ring," she says: "I wondered if it might be Good Book Bob dialing you for dollars again. . ." Once KHVN phoned and asked me who it was said "My stroke is heavier than my groaning." I remembered it was Job because the Book of Job was the only book of the Bible Uncle Dicker ever read aloud to me (he claimed it was to help me reconcile my disfiguremnt but I personally think it was because of him constantly suffering from the rupture) and when I won forty dollars and a representational madonna of unbreakable lucite Miss Lawn never got over it. If I was in the tub or laid down napping and the phone rang more'n once she'd scoot all the way around from her place in time to answer the third ring, just in case it might be another contest. That's how she thinks of me and of what she refers to as my "four-leaf-clover-life." Sometimes she comes in and *waits* for it to ring. She swears up and down that I must be hard of hearing because she *always* knocks before she comes in; all I say is it must be with a gum-rubber knuckle. "Well, it was not Good Book Bob," I assure her: "It was my grandson." "Oh? The *famous* one?" she wants to know. I just nodded and snapped the fieldglasses away in their case before I went on. Very deliberately. "He's coming in a special bus this afternoon to take his grandmother to a big surprise party everybody's giving her." I admit I was rubbing it in a bit but I swear she can aggravate a person. "I'll probably be away to the festivities *all evening*," I says. Her mouth made a little round O: "Be away and miss Reverend Poll's *special service?* and the donuts and the Twylight Towers *Trio?* Mrs. Whittier, you must be delirious!" I told her I was attending another service and instead of those soggy donuts was having a *fantastic* cake. But I didn't have the heart to tell her about the Sounding Brass. Them eyes were already going from red to green like traffic lights. In the entire year and a half she's lived in the apartment next door I do believe the only visits she's had from the outside is Jehova Witnesses and Avon Callings. I says "I *am*, Miss Lawn: dee-*lerious!*" And that I was going to have myself a good long hot soak in Sardo before I *popped* with delirium so, if she would please excuse-a *plize* and went strutting into the bathroom without another word. I like Miss Lawn well enough—we went to the same church for years and got along just fine, except her seeming a little snooty. I thought that came from her being a Lawn of the

Lawn's Sand & Gravel Lawns, a rich old Oregon family and very high society around Eugene. It wasn't till Urban Renewal forced her to follow me to the Towers that I realized what a lonesome soul she actually was. And *jealous*. . . she can't hardly stand how people make over me. She says the way people make over me you'd think I was the only one in the building. I always say well, I don't know about that, but I *am* glad people like me. *Well*, she says, they ought to like *me*; I never done anything to make people *dislike* me! I says all I do is try and be nice and she says Yeah, but you're *too* mushy with them, *gushy*, whether they're good folks or bad; if I have to get friends like that I don't want 'em. Actually, I'm pretty snippy with people but I say Yeah, well, if you're gonna make friends you're gonna make 'em by *loving* thy neighbor, not all the time acting like you're passing judgment on him. Besides, I never ran into anybody I didn't think but *was good folks*, you get deep enough down. And she says, Well, when you been around as much as *me* you sure will find different; something will happen someday and you'll find out that there are *some* people who are rotten *all the way down!* "Then," she says, "we'll see how that mushy love-thy-neighbor way of yours holds up." Forlorn old frogmouth; what other world could she expect with that kind of pessimistic outlook? Like Papa used to say when one of us kids couldn't tie a shoelace or thread a needle or catch a fish though people on both sides were hauling them in hand over fist: It's all in how you hold your mouth. A little later, though, I called out to her that there was a bottle of cold wine in my Fridgedair. Poor frog, I thought as I pulled my tub. I got it just steaming hot as I could stand and got in. The Sounding Brass! The last and of course only other time I'd been fortunate enough to hear them was after Lena left home to marry Daniel. I got so blue that Emerson drove me back to Pine Bluff for a family reunion and on the way back through Colorada took me to the Sunrise Service at the Garden of the Gods where the Brass family absolutely stole the show. Not just for me, either, but to the extent that when they finished and Dr. Graham took the pulpit even *he* was too choked up to preach. He had to bow his head till the Power of their singing subsided. Afterwards Emery told me that the only time he'd ever before experienced such a Revelation in song was once when the electricity had gone off in the Hollywood Bowl and Tennessee Ernie had stood out from the microphones and sung *There's a Wonder-Working Power* unaided, Emerson said, "by any Juice

but the Lord's." The Deacon Emerson Thoreau Whittier traveled
to a lot of shindigs like that. I usually begged off; *some*body
needs to keep track of the farm, I'd say. After the house burned
and we moved into town I come up with other excuses. Like Emerson's driving being so uncertain that it gave me the hiccups.
Which it did, too. But it wasn't just that, nor just cars. It's anything scurrying around, helter and yon; get here, get there; trains,
buses, airplanes; what all. . . Right this minute my lawyers tell
me I am taking a loss of sixty-five dollars a month on my Gas
Check simply by putting off for almost five years getting on a plane
and flying to Little Rock to sign some papers in person. But I don't
know. Consider the lilies, I say, they toil not neither do they spin,
speaking of which I heard my Fridgedair door slam a couple
times as Miss Lawn got over her snit in the other room, then the
lid of my cut-crystal candy dish, then my television come back on.
The poor old frog. When I finally finished my rinse and come out
in my robe it was still on, blaring. Miss Lawn was gone, though, as
was most of the candy I'd planned to take to the kids at the farm
and *all* of the Annie Green Springs!

I recognized my ride the instant it turned the corner into the
parking lot. Even eighteen stories down and before I got out the
field glasses there was no mistaking it. . . all glistening chrome
and gleaming white and five big purple affairs painted on the side
of it in the formation of a flying cross. When I got them into focus
I seen they were birds, beautiful purple birds. It turned and
parked right in the Buses Only and the door opened. I saw get
out first what I could tell immediately was my grandson by his big
shiny forehead. A*nother* trait from his Grandpa's side; all the
Topple men kept their hair to the grave. Then, behind him, bob-
ble-butting out the bus door, come that big-mouthed doughball of
a character from Los Angeles by the name of Otis. Otis is a kind
of full-grown sissy and has always rubbed me the wrongest of any
of my grandson's gang. He stood there, looking at the Towers like
he might buy it. He had on a little black beanie and around his
rump he had strapped a belt with a scabbard. He pulled out a big
long sword and flashed it around his head for the benefit of all.
About the only good I can say about Otis is that he always goes
back to Southern California as soon as our rains start in the fall,
and stays there till they stop. Which is to say he stays away most
of the year, praise the Lord. Watching him parade around Devlin
with that sword I says to myself Uh-huh, *that's* who it was give me

the willies from the other end of the phone! He's supposed to be quite a successful movie producer is I guess why my grandson tolerates him. "Yep, that was who it was," I says. But then, out comes this other fellow. A big fellow, draped in white from crown to toe like an Arab. Oh, he was something! I strained through the glasses to see if I knew him but his face was all a-swirl. In fact, it seemed that he was wrapped in swirl, a kind of slow swirl. He come floating out of that bus door and sailed about in mid-air like he was moving fast and slow at the same time, reached back in the bus door for somebody else then swirling back, opening like a flower as he lit down. I saw he had a little child who was also dressed in white but only in short pants and shirt with nothing over his head. It was quite apparent then that the both of them were of the black race. He set the little child on his shoulder and Otis with his sword and my grandson with his forehead come into the building, out from beneath my sight. But I could imagine it: Miss Prosper the nurse and receptionist craning her neck across her crossword, Mr. Bolen peeking over the top of his *Organic Gardening*, the rest of the lobby loafers looking up from their games. . . I bet you didn't hear so much as a checker move. And when they traipse back through with *me*, mercy! Maybe, I thought, on the way down I'll say, Oh! you all go on I got to check my mail slot in the basement. Then come up the lower lobby steps and like a yellow skunk circle around to the bus or some such. . .

I just had time to snap on the first jewelry my fingers found and get the last clippie out of my hair before there come two quick knocks at my door, then one, then two more followed by this whisper with a phony accent: "Let me in queeck, Varooshka; they are onto us! Ve must atomize the feelm!" It was that nitwit Otis, of course. I shudder to think what would have happened had he pulled that at Mr. Firestone's door by mistake. I opened as far as the chain would let me and seen it was just a wooden stage sword painted silver. He was wearing those same patched up baggy pants. "I'm sorry," I says: "but I gave all my old rags to the other girl," and slammed it. I heard them all talking. I opened back up and exclaimed "It's *not* the Eastern Star Scrap Drive after all? *I'm* sorry. . ." They laughed at that. "Happy Birthday," Devlin says, hugging me. "You remember Otis Kone?" I took Otis' hand: "Sure." I give it a good squeeze, too. "Sure I remember Otis Kone. Otis comes up from California every summer to try and get my goat." To which Otis says "It's not your goat I'm after, Granny," wiggling his eyebrows, then made like to reach for my necklace. "It's your *gold!*" And I spronged his fat little fingers with a clippie, harder'n I meant. He howled and duckfooted around the hall like Groucho with his fly unzipped. He was still waving that sword but you can tell I took the vinegar out of him. I told him to get his pointed head in out of the hall before somebody called the Humane Society and it was't my gold but *him* who got got. "Point well putten," he says and slunk past so low I had to laugh in spite of myself. He is a clown. I was about to apologize for ragging him when the third fellow glides into sight; "Grandma; this is my long, longtime friend, M'kehla," Devlin says: "and his manchild, Toby." "Mrs. . . . ?" he asks. I tell him it's Whittier and he bows and says "It's Montgomery Keller-Brown, Mrs. Whittier. M'kehla was. . . what would you say, Dev? a phase?" Then he smiles back at me and holds out his hand: "Everyone has told me about Great Grandma. I'm very pleased to meet an obviously beautiful soul."

He was even grander than through the field glasses; tall, elegant, straightbacked and steady-eyed and features like the grains in a polished wood, a rare hardwood, from some far-off land (though I could tell by his voice he was as American as southern and probably as country born as I was). Most of all, though, with a set to his deep dark eyes like I never saw on another earthly being. It wasn't just that he didn't blink; lawyers can look at you without blinking. But this fellow was looking at you all the way from the center of the earth! I found myself fiddling at my collarbuttons and mumbling howdy like a little girl.

"And this," he says, grinning at my fluster, "is October."

Relieved, I let go the hand and looked to the little feller. About four years old and cute as a bug, squinting up at me from the folds in his daddy's robe. "Was that when you was born, honey? October?" I'm used to how little kids first take how I look, but his daddy says, "Answer Mrs. Whittier, October." I says "It's all right; October don't know if this ugly old woman is a good witch who's going to give him one of her taffy-babies or a bad witch gonna eat him up," and stuck my false teeth out at him. That usually gets them. "Toby," he answers, stepping out of the shrouds and opening up—he didn't smile though—and unsquinting his eyes so it was then I seen. "Toby is the name I like best." Luckily I managed not to let on. "Okay, Toby; let's get some candy before that Otis consumes it all." We all come in and chatted about my apartment and the P.P.H. program. I let little Toby look through the field glasses while my grandson showed me a little program of what was happening today. I said it looked like it was going to be a real nice affair. Otis dug down into one of his big pockets and come up with a handbill of his own that said "ARE YOU PREPARED?" with a picture of him in a priest's outfit. He was looking up at the sky through the tube out of a roll of toilet tissue, his mouth saying in big black letters "THE CHICKEN-WIRE PARACHUTE IS COMING." I knew it was just more of Otis' nonsense but I folded it up put it in my overnight bag and told him I was *always* prepared. And that I notice *he* is, *too*, and reach down like to zip up his baggy old pants. He turns his back to do it himself, his ears are red as peppers. *Some*body's got to teach these city kids, I tell Mr. Keller-Brown and he laughs soft and deep and warm. My grandson looks over my bag, hefts at the straps and says "Uhn; who do you usually get to carry your purse?" I told him "Now don't you razz a woman about her essentials," and if he didn't think he was stout enough to handle it I bet little Toby could. The little boy put the glasses right down and come and started to lug at the purse. "Give that here," I says, "I was just spoofin'. But aint we the good little helper, though?" Mr. Keller-Brown takes the bag and smiles down at the serious little face: "We work on being the good little helper, don't we, Tobe?" and the little fellow nodded back, "Yes, daddy," and I couldn't help but think what a change from most of the little kids you see being let go hog wild these days, what a gratifying change.

I locked my door and followed them down to the elevator, my grandson and Mr. Keller-Brown on either side escorting me and Otis skipping along ahead with the child by the hand. The main elevator was still being used to clear out the collection of metal they found when they opened poor Mr. Fry's apartment, so we had some wait for the other one which didn't go to the basement. I said I hoped we didn't miss the Brass family. Devlin says we got plenty of time. He said did I know that Mr. Keller-Brown was part of a gospel singing group himself? Quite popular, too, he said. I says Oh? what are you called? Because I might have heard them on KHVN. Mr. Keller-Brown says they were called the Birds of Prayer but he doubted I'd heard them, not on AM. Then him and Devlin started talking about what an idea it would be to next year *broadcast* the Worship over FM closed circuit this and that on

112

into technicalities till I couldn't keep track. Also, that Otis was so distracting, clowning around for Toby, pretending to pick berries off the plastic philodendron and pop them in his mouth. The little fellow was obediently standing for it but you could tell he wished his hand was loose. The elevator arrived with Mrs. Kennicut from 19 and the two Birwell sisters. When I told them good afternoon I was escorted on by a big black Arab, a forty-year-old pink-pated hippy, a dough-white sword-toting toadstool, and a child of too many hues, you could have knocked their eyes off with a broomstick. Otis gave them each one of his handbills, too. Nobody says a thing. We went down a few floors where a maintenance man pushed on carrying a big pry bar much to Mrs. Kennicut's very apparent relief. He don't say anything, either, but he hefts his pinch bar to his shoulder like a club. So nothing will do but Otis take out his sword and hold it on his shoulder, too. We slid on down, packed tight and tense. I thought Boy, is *this* gonna cause a stink around me for months to come. With that sword every neighbor I got will think I'm being kidnapped. Shanghaied. By a gang of those elements Paul Harvey warns you preys on Senior Citizens. Or that I'm *one* of them, an inside contact. I know this sounds silly but I also know how lots of these poor scared folks think. What with Watergate at one end and the muggers on the other, one more straw's all it would take. I was racking my head for some way to ease the shock or leastwise disassociate from it when, from below, I felt this little hand slip up into mine and heard a little voice say, "It's crowdy, Grandma. Pick me up." And I lifted him up, and held him on my hip the rest of the ride down, and carried him right on out through that lobby, black curls, brown skin, blue eyes and all.

I seen some rigs around Eugene—remodeled trailers and elegrant hippy buses and whatnot—but I never saw anything on wheels the beat of this outfit of Mr. Keller-Brown's. Ivory white it was painted, and I don't mean by some amateur with a can of enamel and a brush; a sheen like that was a professional's work. Class-y, I told Mr. Keller-Brown, and was it ever. From the five purple birds on the side right down to the little chrome cross hood ornament. This, in*side:* I swear it was like the living room of a traveling palace: tapestries, moldings, a tile floor, even a little stone fireplace! All I could do was gape goggle-eyed. "I just helped minimumly," he explained; "My wife is the one that put it together." I told him he must have quite *some wife* to build all those cabinets and bookcases. Otis puts in that Montgomery Keller-Brown did indeed have quite some wife, plus that his wife had quite some father, who had quite some chain of restaurants and quite some bank account. . . which might have helped minimumly as well. I watched to see how Mr. Keller-Brown was going to take this. It must be touchy enough for a Negro man to be married to a white girl; and if she's rich to *boot*. . . But he just laughed and winked at me and led me toward the rear and said with his mouth *sour grapes*. "Devlin told me about your back. I've got a chair here I think might suit you; a therapeutic recline-o-lounger. . ." He pushed back a big leather chair: "Or, there's the bed," then ran his hand over a deep purple wool bedspread on a king-sized bed fixed right into the back of the bus. "Fiddlesticks," I says. "I hope it *never* gets to where I'm not capable of sitting in a chair like a human." He said I looked plenty capable to him. His voice was as rich as his furniture, and deep. "And shoot on you, Devlin, telling tales about my back *behind* my back! I'll sit here a while then maybe I'll lay on that bed a while, as my fancy takes me!" He took my arm and helped me into the chair, my face burning like a beet. "And what are *you* grinning at, Otis? Fool with me and *I'll drive* this hoppy. Then where'd you be?" I leaned back, pulled my dress down over my legs and asked them what they were waiting on, anyhow. I could feel twenty stories of wrinkled old noses pressed to their windows as we drove out of the lot. Toby set down at a little desk with crayolas and Otis piddled with the tape machine. The bus grumbled along. I could feel my silly puss still burning and everybody waiting for me to say something so I hollered at Mr. Keller-Brown's face in the rearview that I guessed it would get us there without coming apart so go ahead and get it outta low. He grinned and hollered back Thanks. To my way of thinking it's harder to be made over special than the other way around. I never could see how those people stood for it on "This Is Your Life."

Me and my grandson gossiped a bit about what was happening with the family, especially Buddy, who seemed to be getting in two messes with his dairy business as quick as he got out of one. Up front, Otis had found a pint bottle of hooch from one of his big baggy pockets and was trying to share it with the driver. Devlin saw the bottle and hemmed and hawed and said maybe he'd better go up front; to make sure that addlehead doesn't direct us to *Alaska* or something, he says. I told him Phooey! I didn't care if they drunk the whole bottle and all three fell out the door; Toby and me could handle things! Devlin swayed away up to the front and pretty soon the three men were talking a mile a minute. The little boy eased out of his desk and sidled back to where I was. He took a *National Geographic* out of the bookcase and made like to get himself comfortable on the floor beside my chair. I smiled my nicest look at him and waited. Pretty quick his big blue eyes came up over the top of the book and I said peek-a-boo. Without another word he put he book down and crawled right up into my lap. "Did Jesus do that to your face?" he asks me. I says "Why, don't tell me you're the *only* boy who never heard what Tricker the Squirrel done for the Toad?" And went into the tale about how Mr. Toad used to be very very beautiful in the olden times with a face so lovely that it shined like a green jewel and kept showing the bugs where he was laid in wait for them. "He would have starved if it wasn't for Tricker camouflaging him with warts, don'cher see?" He nodded, solemn but satisfied, and asks me to tell him another one. I started in about Tricker and the Bear called Big Double but he went off to sleep with one hand holding mine and the other hanging onto my cameo pendant. Which was just as well because the therapeutic recline-o-lounger was about to kill me. I unclasped the chain and slipped out from under him and the locket both. The deep philosophic discussion going on at the front of the bus never skipped a beat. I backed over to the bed and sunk down into that purple wool very near out of sight. It was one of those waterbeds, and it had me like quicksand only my feet waggling up over the edge. Very unladylike. But wiggle and waggle as I might I could not get back up. Every time I got to an elbow the bus would turn and I would be washed down again. I reminded myself of a fat old ewe we used to have who would lose her balance grazing on a slope and roll over and have to lay there bleating with her feet in their air till somebody turned her back right side up. I gave up floundering and let the water slosh to and fro under me while I looked over the selection in Mr. Keller-Brown's bookcase by the bed. Books on every crazy thing you ever heard of, religions and pyramids and mesmerism and the like. Lots with foreign titles and some even with foreign letters. looking at the books and listening to the three of them up there talking ten miles above my head made me uneasy. Actually, I was feeling fine. If there'd been a TV man there I could've peddled a thousand of those waterbeds. "Feel twenty years younger! Like

115

a New Woman! I had to giggle; all the driver had to do was look in that mirror and see the new woman's runny old nylons sticking spraddled into the air like the hindquarters of a stranded sheep. And while I was thinking about it it seemed I felt sure enough a heavy dark look brush me, like an actual touch, Lord, like an actual physical presence.

The next I know we were pulling into the old Nebo place. Devlin was squeezing my foot. "Thought for a minute you'd passed on," he teased. He took my arm to help me out of the bed. I told him I'd thought so for a while, too, till I saw that familiar old barn go by the bus window. "Then I knew I wasn't in no Great Beyond." He laughed and the bus stopped and I sit down and put on my shoes. Mr. Keller-Brown came back and ask me how my nap was. "I'm fresh as a daisy," I told him. "I never had such a relaxing ride. Devlin, you put one of the waterbeds in your convertible and I just might go galavantin'." Mr. Keller-Brown says, Well, they were going to drive to Los Angeles to sing Sunday morn and he would sure be proud to have me come along. I told him if things kept going my way like they had been I just might consider it. Little Toby says "Oh *do*, Grandma; do come with us." I said all right I *would* consider it. He kept on begging me till Mr. Keller-Brown scooped him up from the recline-o-lounger. He still had a-holt of my pendant. "What's this?" Mr. Keller-Brown asks. He has to pry it from the little tyke's fingers. "Don't you think we better give this back to Mrs. Whittier, Tobe?" He hands me the necklace but I go over and open the little desk top and drop it in amongst the crayolas. "It's Toby's, I told them, "not mine." I said an angel came down and give it to Toby in his dreams. Toby nods somber as an owl and says Yeah, Daddy, a angel, and adds —because of the cameo face on it was all I could think—"A *white* angel." Then Otis hollers "Let's boogie for Jesus!" and we all go out. We'd parked kind of on the road because the parking area (what *used* to be our permanent pasture of clover and timothy) was full to overflowing, cars, buses, campers, and every sort of thing. The Worship Fair was going like a three-ring circus, people thick as hair on a dog around, arguing, singing. A long-haired skinny young fellow without shoes or shirt was clamping a flyer under every windshield wiper and a ways behind him another long-hair sticking CHRIST'S THE ONE to the bumpers was sneaking off the fiiers when the first kid wasn't looking. Otis went over with his sword to straighten it all out and pass out some fliers of his own. Across the orchard I could see they'd built a stage on the foundations where the house used to stand. At the microphone a nervous young girl was playing a sourish zither and singing scripture in a nervous shaky voice. Devlin asks me if I knew the verse she was singing and playing. Otis says he thought the singing vas verse than the playing, but it vas a toss-up. I says I didn't know. For one thing the dust in that parking lot was about to stifle me. Mr. Keller-Brown says it was the sixty-sixth Psalm and I said Oh no! The sixty-sixth Psalm is Make a Joyful Noise Unto God All You Lands. . . what she's singing is from Isiah. And was about to name the verse, too, but he smiles down on me with that look and says "It depends on your translation, Mrs. Whittier. King James was a wellknown Deceiver." I knew I was out of my water so I hushed up. I never even argued with Emerson T. when he got off on those finer points. It did strike me strange, though, that neither Devlin nor Otis took issue. . .

Back behind the stage we found Betsy and the kids. They wanted to give me my presents right off but Betsy told them to wait for the cake. The men went off to take care of getting the next act on stage and I went off with Betsy and the kids to look how their garden was coming up. Caleb led Toby on ahead through the gate hollering "I'll show *you* something, Toby." Betsy told me that the mama siamese had her nest in the rhubarb; "She just had one kitten. She had six hidden out in the haybarn but Devlin backed the tractor over five of them. She brought the last one into the garden. He's old enough to wean but that mama cat just won't let him out of the rhubarb." We strolled along, looking how high the peas were already and how the perennials had stood the big freeze and when we got to the rhubarb there was little Toby amongst the leaves hugging the kitten and grinning for all he was worth. "That's the first time I seen the little scoot smile," I told Betsy. "Toby can't have our kitten, can he, Mom?" Caleb asks. Betsy says if it's all right with his folks it was most decidedly all right with her. I said with all the traffic maybe we'd better leave the kitty in the garden until he asks his mama. The smile went away but he didn't turn loose. He stood there giving us a look that would have tugged a top sargeant's heart. Betsy said he could carry it if he was careful. "We'll ask M'kehla," she says. All the rest of the afternoon Toby hung onto that cat for dear life, Caleb worrying at him from one side and the anxious mama cat from the other.

Sherree took me in to show me her new curtains and we all had some coffee. We could hear things getting worked up. We mosied back to the stage just as an all-boy chorus from Utah was finishing up. People had commenced to push in towards the stage and it was pretty thick, but the kids saved me a nice shady spot with a blanket and some of those tie-dyed pillows. I didn't see Devlin or Mr. Keller-Brown but Otis was impossible to miss. He was reeling around in front of the stage making a real spectacle of himself, getting all tripped up in his sword which was worked round between his legs: "Hallelujah I *believe!* I forget in what but brethren and sistren I *believe.* . ." He had his shirt off and his flubbery old belly was red as a lobster. He was too looped to care, I guess, hollering Hallelujah and Amen and Remember Pearl Harbor. And somebody had spray-painted across the rump of his baggy pants: "The Other Cheek." I told Betsy he hadn't better turn that other cheek to *me* if he knew what was good for him. The announcer was one of the local ministers. He looked about as pleased with the proceedings as Mr. Firestone would have. After the all-boys from Utah he asked if we couldn't have a little quiet and a little respect—he said this right at Otis, too—"a little respect for one of the all-time great gospel groups of all time: The Sounding Brass!" Just like they made their entrance in Colorada Springs a gong was rung back stage, soft and slow at first, then faster and faster louder and louder and louder. Even Otis set down. The gonging rose and rose until you thought the sky would open and when you thought you couldn't stand it a moment more made one last hard loud bang and they came running on stage and went right into *Ring Them Bells.*

At first I thought, Why, I been tricked! The Sounding Brass? these five old butterballs? The Sounding Brass is tall and lean with natural red hair that shines like five halos, not these sorry old jokes. Why, the men didn't have a hundred scraggly old white hairs divided between the four of them. And the woman was wearing a wig that looked like it had been made out of wire and rusted. And I'm darned if she didn't have on a mini-dress, I could see the veins from fifty feet away. I just shook my head. It was them all right. All their movements and gestures were exactly those I remembered, but it looked like they'd been set to moving and then forgot the grease. And their voices were just horrible. I don't mean old—I know a lot of older groups who sing fine, creaks whistles and all—I mean *thin, hollow,* like whatever had been there had been scraped away and left five empty shells. I read how they'd had a lot of income tax problems; maybe that done it. But they were surely pathetic. They finished a couple of songs and people give them a little hand of pure charity. Then Jacob Brass stepped to the microphone and says "Now. We *hear* from *reliable sources* that this next number is the *favorite* of a very fine lady out there having her birthday on this beautiful spring day. *Eighty-six years young!* This Good Friday song is dedicated to that Good Friday Birthday Girl!" I wanted to dig a hole and crawl in it. And, let me tell you; if they sounded bad on their faster numbers now they sounded downright pitiful. Also, to make matters worse that dad-blamed Otis got going again, answering back. They'd sing "Were you there. . . when they nailed Him to the cross?" and Otis would yell out "Not me, youse mugs! I was in Tarzana drinking Orange Juliuses I can prove it!" loud enough the people got to laughing. Which of course only encouraged him. "Pierced Him in the *side?* Ech. I wasn't there *then,* either. I don't even go t'roller derby." The Brass family was so peeved by the laughter that to the secret relief of all they stalked off stage as soon as they finished two choruses, absolutely furious. "Why were they so mad," Toby asked, and Caleb whispers, "Cause they saw you were stealing our kitten." Betsy says Caleb! but Toby ignores him completely and tells me to get ready, Grandma because here come his folks. *Then* did the crowd hoop and holler! The Birds of Prayer was the other end of the stick from the Brass family. They pranced out all in purple, Mr. Keller-Brown and another big black fellow with a beard, and sung bass, and Mr. Keller-Brown played those big native drums and kind of come in now and then, talking to them. The three colored girls sung and shook tambourines. After the Brass family these kids were like a breath of fresh air. My grandson comes through the crowd toward us, bouncing up and down to the rhythm. "How do you like them?" he asks, taking a pillow alongside me. I told him they were as good as anything I ever heard on KHVN but I thought somebody said Mr. Keller-Brown's wife was one of the group. He says "She is. That's her on the left." And before I thought I says "But what about our blue-eyed little—" I stopped but I'd said enough. I could have bit my stupid tongue off.

Then the next thing that happened was after sundown. After the service which was I thought prudently short, and after the main of the crowd drove away or drifted off with sleeping bags to little campfires, a bunch of us walked down to the ash grove for my cake. Mr. Keller-Brown had pulled his bus down there and the kids had set up a table in front of it where the cake was waiting. They sung Happy Birthday, Great Grandma while Quiston scampered around with a box of matches trying to keep all those candles lit. "Here!" says I; "you kids help Grandma blow 'em out before we start the woods a-blaze." There was Devlin's three, Buddy's two, some of their chums, and in the back outside this ring of glowing faces he stood still holding that cat. "Let Toby in there, Quiston. This many candles gonna need all the breath we can muster. Okay everybody? one. . . two. . . " with all of them drawing a lungful except him there, his chin resting between the ears of that siamese kitty both of them looking right at me, expressions absolutely the same. "Blow!" When I could see again his daddy was standing where he'd stood, lighting a Coleman lantern. He'd changed out of his purple jump suit into his most spectacular outfit so far. "Goodness me! Aren't you something! You're almost as pretty as this cake. . . Actually, the cake looked like one of them lumpy tie-dye pillows whereas his robe was an absolutely beautiful affair, purple velvet and gold trim, absolutely wriggling front and back with some of the finest needlepoint I ever saw—dragons, and eagles, and bulls you could practically hear snorting as he thanked me kindly and did a slow swirl with the lantern held up hissing above him. "You must've locked your little woman home with needle and thread for about six months," I says. I'd had a glass of sherry with Betsy before and was feeling feisty. "Nope," he says, starting to ladle out papercups of punch for the kids; "It only took three months. And l'l ol' *me* made it." This last he says in the high, simpering voice of a little pickyninny girl to a T and swirls once more around, very delicate for a man. "I *knew*," I says, just aiming to fun him a bit; "that it wasn't the work of no *man*." The kids all laughed again but he took it some way wrong, and the laugh died off too quick. Instead of responding to my rib he went back to handing out that punch. To try to smooth over my foolishness I says "Go on. I bet your wife *did too* sew it." By way of apology. But before he could accept my effort Otis stumbles up and butts across in front of us to take a dixiecup and says "Oh I'll vouch for M'kehla's wife, Grandma; she doesn't make *any*thing. . ." He pours the cup about half full of brandy before he adds: "Hardly." The quiet got even quieter. I thought he was going to look two holes in the top of Otis's head. But Otis keeps sniffing his nose down in his booze like he don't notice a thing. "Brandy from a dixiecup," he moans; "How hast they chalice shrunk, Lawd." Sherree starts slicing the cake but the kids hang back. Toby watches his daddy and Otis. Otis just kept a-snipping on: "Thy wafer has *swollen* to at least four-hundred calories, Lawd, but they grail is *waxpaper!* Tut tut and tut. At my bah mitsvah we drank from at *least* clear plastic. . ." Otis had got worse and worse after his success aping the Brass family, singing and reciting and cutting up, stripping finally clear down to his dingy shorts his sword and the little cap he wore. Yet everybody had took it in good humor. He was a nuisance but after a while you saw he couldn't help it. Devlin told me once that Otis was like he was because he'd been given too much oxygen at birth, so nobody ever really took offense at what he said. But Mr. Keller-Brown was still brooding, set off by that goof of mine, I guess, because he reached out and took the papercup out of Otis' hand and says "Is this your first communion, Mr. Kone? We'll just have to get something more fitting for your first communion. . ." I noticed Betsy stop dipping ice cream. And back by the campfire his wife's sister stood up from where she'd been talking with my two grandsons and Claude Muddle's wife, Blanch. Mr. Keller-Brown says "If you'll take my ladle, Mrs. Whittier, I'll see if we can't find Mr. Kone a more appropriate vessel." His wife's sister comes hurrying over and says "I'll get it, Montgomery——" but he says No, he'd do it, and she stops on a dime. Otis reaches for the cup mumbling something about not to trouble and he says No, it's no trouble, Mr. Kone, and Otis's hand stops just the same way. He still hasn't looked up to Mr. Keller-Brown's eyes. The kids are beginning to get upset so I say, "Why, if Mr. Kone gets a glass to drink out of, Mr. Keller-Brown, oughten *I* get a glass to drink out of?" Little Sherree, who is a Libra and a smart little peacemaker in her own right, joins in and says "Yeah, it's Great *Grand*ma's birthday." And the other kids and Toby, too, says yeah grandma gets a glass, too! Those eyes lift off Otis and move to me. "Certainly," he says, laughing off his temper, "Forgive me, Mrs. Whittier." He winked to me and jerked his thumb back at Otis by way of explanation. I winked and nodded back to indicate I knew precisely what he meant, that many's the time I wanted to wring that jellyroll's neck myself. Smiling, he went into the bus and the kids went back at the cake and ice cream. I never could stand having people fight around me. I've always been handy at oiling troubled waters. Like when I was living with Lena: Devlin and Buddy would get in terrible squabbles over whose turn it was to mow the lawn. While they were fussing I'd go get the lawn mower and mow away till they come sheepfaced out to take over (more handy than straightforward, to be honest). So I thought the storm was past when Mr. Keller-Brown come back out with three dusty brandy glasses and shared some of Otis's brandy. I blew at the dust and filled mine with the kid's punch and all of us clinked glasses and toasted my birthday. Otis said that he could sympathize with me, being eighty-sixed quite a number of times himself. Everybody laughed and he was down from the hook. Five minutes later he was running off at the mouth as bad as ever.

I opened my little pretties and doo-dads the kids had made me and give them all a big hug. Buddy rolled some logs up to the fire. We sat about and sung a few songs while the kids roasted marshmellows. Claude Muddle stamped around playing the mouth harp while the big black fellow with the beard patted at Mr. Keller-Brown's drums. Devlin strummed the guitar though he never could play worth sour apples. The fire burnt down and the moon come up through the new ash leaves. Betsy and Buddy's wife took their kids up to the house. Mr. Keller-Brown took Toby into the hut, him still hugging the kitty. He brought out a jar of little pellets that he sprinkled into the embers. Real myrrh, he said, from Lebanon. It smelled fresh and sharp, like cedar pitch on a warm fall wind, not sickening sweet like other incense. Then he brought out some pillows and the men settled down to discussing the workings of the universe and I knew it was time for me to go to bed. "Where's that giant purse of mine?" I whispered to my grandson. He says "It's in the cabin. Betsy has made the bed for you. I'll walk you up that way." I told him Never mind; that the moon was bright and I could walk my way around this territory with a blindfold on anyway, and told them all goodnight. The crickets were singing in the ash trees, happy that summer was here. I passed Emerson's old plow; somebody had set out to weld it into a mailbox stand and had apparently give up and just left it rust in the weeds, half plow and half mailbox and no longer good for neither. It made me sad and I noticed the crickets had hushed. I was taking my time, almost to the fence, when he was suddenly in front of me—a sharp black pyramid in the moonlight, those two eyes boring down at me, hissing: "Backdoor! Don't you never come slippin' in the backdoor on *my* little boy again, y'understand? *never!* That necklace I let pass 'cause I say 'She old. She don't know.' But then to pull the same bullshit about the mother-fucking *cat*. . . that's backdoor!'" Two big hands from some-body behind grabbed both sides of my head. I though they was going to crush my cranium! I couldn't holler or turn aside or even blink. "White angel, my ass! *I* show *you*, white angel!" It was like he pulled back the black blouse of his face and two breasts come straining out towards me swirling and drooping out and down until the black nipples touched my very eyeballs. . . giv-ing suck. . . milking into me such thoughts and pictures that my mind knew at once not to think about or look at. Let them slide, I said, sli-i-ide. . . and I made a picture of rain falling on a duck. This duck splattering around must have come as a shock to him because he blinked. I felt the invisible hands drop from my head and I knew there hadn't been nobody behind me. "So don't let me catch you—" The duck run out a great long neck and quacked. He fumbled and blinked again. "Don't try no secret influence on my *son* again, is all I wanted to tell you. Y'understand? You un-derstand? A dude, a father's got to look out for his own." And was gone back in the bush before I could catch my breath to an-swer. I hotfooted right on up to the cabin *then* I hope to tell you! And without slowing one iota pulled the shades took two yellow pills got in bed and yanked the covers up over my head. I didn't dare think. I recited in my mind all the scripture I knew, and *My Country Tis of Thee*, and *O Say Can You See*, and I was into bread recipes before they took effect.

Just like praying for something, Lord, I don't like to take a pill unless it's absolutely necessary. Often's the night I laid awake till dawn listening to the elevators go up and down the Towers than take one of these blessed pills. They always make me sleep too long and wake up feeling dopey as a dog and can't really see clear for a couple of days. Plus you don't even dream, usually. But now I found myself dreaming like a fire broke out. It was those thoughts and pictures I'd been fed. I hadn't shed them after all. I'd just covered them over like sparks in a mattress. Now they were blazing to life in my dream. . . Mainly it was this shadow thing—sometimes it was an alligator, sometimes it was a panther or a wolf—rushing through my world and snapping off pieces, all the weak namby-pamby limbs, like snapping off Devlin's hands playing the guitar, or Claude Muddle's leg while he was striding around, or my tongue from saying little oil-on-the water fibs. Miss Lawn it lopped off absolutely. And Emerson T., and most of my past. Then it moved ahead, a dark pruning shadow mowing through the years and years ahead until only the bare bones of a future was left naked, with no more fibs, nor birthday cakes, nor presents and doo-dads for ever and evermore. Standing there. And out of this naked thing the heat began to drain, till the ground was as warm as the soles of its feet and the wind the same temperature as its breathing. It still *was* but its was was no more than the rock's or the wind's and all it could do was to stand there gawking into eternity waiting in case God might want to use it again. Like an old mule or the ghost of a mule, its meaning spent, its furrows gone to the tractor, its seed never planted and wouldn't have grown anyway because it is a mule, a trick of God. It saddened me to my very marrow. It seemed I could hear it braying its terrible bleak lonesomeness forever. I wept for it and wished I could say something; but how can you offer comfort to one of the bleak tricks of God? It brayed louder. Not so bleak, now, nor far off sounding, and I opened my eyes and sat up in bed. Out the window I saw Otis under the moon, howling and running in circles in his bloody shorts crazy as a loon. Devlin and the others were trying to get him but he still had his wooden sword and was slashing at them: "Keep your place. It wasn't me not this wienie *he had no call!* Devlin? Claude? Help me old chums, he he's put the glacier on your old *he had no justifications to prune I'm already done!*" First begging for help then whacking at them when they came close screaming like they'd turned into monsters. "He's trimming me, boys, dontcha see? Me who never so much as *he had no right you black bastards* AAAAHH!" And get so wound up he'd scream and run right into the fence around the chicken yard. He'd bounce off the fence and hew the men back away from him and carry on and cuss at them till he had to howl and run into the wire again. The chickens were squawking the men hollering and Otis I tell you truly was going plumb mad. This isn't no foolishness, I told myself; this is simon pure unvarnished *madness!* He needs *help!* But I just watched like it was more of the same dream rushing about in the moonlight and chicken feathers, until Otis got his sword snaffled in the wire and the men swarmed on him. They carried him thrashing and weeping to the house right past my cabin window. He was covered from the neck to the knees in a chicken wire print. As soon as they were gone from sight I was up out of that bed. Without a further thought on the matter I put on my housecoat and slippers and struck out toward the ash grove.

I wasn't scared, exactly. The ground seemed to be heaving, the trees was full of faces and every witchdoctor and conjure-man story I ever heard was tumbling up out of my spooky Ozark childhood to keep me company, but I still wasn't scared. Maybe I suspicioned if I let myself get the slightest bit scared I'd be raving worse than Otis.

He wasn't sticking pins in dolls, though. He was sitting in the therapeutic recline-o-lounger reading out of his big books by the light of the Coleman lamp, a big pair of earphones on his head. There was a tape or record or some such playing, of a bunch of men's voices chanting in a foreign tongue. His mouth was moving to the words of the chant as he read. I slapped on the side of the bus and ask up the stairwell, Hello. . . can I come in a minute? "Mrs. Whittier?" he says and comes to the door. "*Sure*, man. Come on in. I'm honored." He gives me his hand and seems genuinely happy to see me. I told him I had been thinking and if there'd been a misunderstanding but he cuts right in, apologizing like sixty how he'd acted abominable and unexcusable and hang on a second. He held up a big palm asking me to wait while he swirled around to flip a switch on his phonograph. The speakers went off but the tape still turned on the machine and I could still hear a tiny chorus chanting out of the earphones in the recline-o-lounger: Rah. Rah. Rah ree run. "I'm glad you come," he says. "For real. I been feeling terrible for the way I acted. There was no excuse for it and I apologize for getting so heavy on you." I told him it was understandable, and that was why I was there. I started to tell him that I had never said anything about the kitty when I glanced back to the waterbed. She still wasn't there but the little boy was, lying propped up on a pillow like a ventriloquist doll eyes staring at a glass bead strung from the ceiling. He had on his own pair of earphones, and the bead twisted and untwisted.

"Well I get to apologize first," I told Mr. Keller-Brown. That was why I'd come. I told him that he'd been completely correct, and that I had no right telling his child those kind of whoppers and *deserved* a scolding. The chant went something like Rah. Rah. Tut nee cum. Cum cum eye sis rah. Mr. Keller-Brown says okay, we've traded apologies. Gimmee some skin and we're chums again. I said I was glad I got it off my chest. Rah. Rah. Tut nee eye sis rah sum *rah* and that bead turning slow as syrup on its thread. He says he hopes I'll still consider riding down to LA with them; they'd be honored. I says we'll see how I feel tomorrow;

it's been a big day. He says goodnight and helps me back down the steps. I thank him. At the bus window waving his face gives me no clue whether he believed it or not. I smiled and waved back. A few steps later I knew I had convinced him. Everything suddenly turned ten times brighter as I felt him withdraw that terrible pruning shadow and return it to its sheath. Now forget it I told myself, all, and made a picture of the rain stopping and the duck flying off. The look of things was headed back to normal. There were crickets in the trees; nothing else. The ground ran level and the night was calm. I had just about convinced myself that it was all over, that it was all just a widder woman's nightmare, nothing more, nothing worse, when I heard the mama siamese meowing.

The kitten was stuffed under some ash roots and covered with big rocks. I could barely move them. You were right, I told the mama cat; you should've kept him in the rhubarb. You knew when you seen all those cars and motorcycles and buses zooming around it was no place for a little kitty. She followed crying as I carried it up to the cabin. I kept talking to her as I walked, and fingering the poor stiffening little kitty to see if it was cut or broke or what, and when I found it I was reminded of the time I was picking pears in the dusk as a kid of a girl in Penrose, Colorada, and reached up to get what I thought was sure a funny fuzzy feeling pear before it uncurled and squeaked and flew away and I fell off the ladder with bat bites all over my hand. . . was what I thought as my fingers recognized the cameo and found the chain knotted around its neck. O *Lord*, I cried, what have I got into and carried it on into the cabin and got right down on my knees to You for a sign what now

Her eyes opened and her face raised again. Now the moonlight glanced across its ridges and gullies. She drew a long breath and picked up the kitten and closed it in a drawer. Her hands were shaking so she could barely open the bottle of nembutal. Before she fell asleep she heard the first rooster crow. *If not a sign Lord Jesus to make me certain then how about the strength to act like i am for it looks to me like i am left with no choice but to go ahead a shield a fortress a harbor Amen Lord amen*

# PART TWO

*Prayer Two: Holy Saturday*

*contrary to promises previous its Your old gal friend once again
Only-Begotten airing another classified help-wanted actually
needed in fact rather desperately and o dear Lord pardon me that
this airing might seem a whiff pickiunish when i specify its not
no Angel nor Heavenly Spirit im advertising after but a earthly
ally and also excuse me if this next smells of disrespect and even
blasphemy still i have to say Lord that when You told us up on the
Mount of Olives how we would have to take careful heed that nobody deceive us then prophesied how there will be many who
would come in Your Name to do precisely that and succeed too
with a majority of ordinary folks then went on to tell how in our
last days false prophets would come and show great signs and
wonders fashioned so slick as to deceive not only the ordinary hoi
polloy but the very elect as well that you might have also gone
ahead and told us some signals specifically like the seven danger
signs of cancer to keep our eye peeled for so a fella could take
that heed you suggest more carefully and in time to cull out those
diseased specimens before the whole barrel is spoilt but most of
all Anointed Saviour for what might be no is bound to be the rud-
est most thankless affront of all if indeed i am guilty of it please
forgive me if what i have to say stinks rudely of rank ingratitude
as i fear it must for though i know Martyred Lamb know and
deeply believe when You died on the cross for mankinds sins You
not only redeemed us but You most assuredly did return to us as
promised in that shining beacon of a blessing the priceless gift of
the Spirit of Truth which i previous to this predicament always
considered ample illumination to reveal all and sundry that this
simple headbusted busybody would ever need to know about the
heart of any matter concerning her personally or her family barrel
in general but maybe like miss lawn said maybe i been able to
maintain my rose-colored outlook this long only because i never
previous come across anybody i ever really suspicioned might be
rotten to the core and now that i have if indeed i have i admit to*

*needing more aid than Your blessed Inpeering Light of Truth*
*Lord to help me peel away the uncertainty. I confess as well to*
*needing more support than signs. Not that i am ungrateful for the*
*signs. Signs are fun like Good Book Bob's Christmas Crosswords*
*Clues, but not fully adequate unless there's a full follow-up of*
*answers printed tomorrow. Without the next edition's follow-up,*
*Lord, shedding light, I'm afraid signs and clues make mainly for*
*suspicion more than illumination. Shades of doubt are bound to*
*creep back without a confirmation. After while, in the creep of*
*enough of these shadows, a feller don't know whether to suspect*
*the suspect, or the suspector. This must have been what she meant*
*sure enough, that Miss Lawn: suspicion without confirmation*
*eventually points the finger both ways so it thereby suspects its*
*ownself without it has somebody to corroborate it from outside the*
*two-ended aim of that dadgummed finger . . . from outside not*
*above because at the risk of even ingratitude, Sweet Redeemer, I*
*must in all honesty say that while Your Spirit of Truth is a price-*
*less light to one's own insides it don't reveal the inside of anything*
*outside worth beans if the thing outside is firmly adamantly bent*
*on keeping its insides concealed and if in the long run a fella can't*
*be sure of the inside of something outside how in the long run*

Her head came up abruptly. Her lips stopped and her eyes
opened and she sat face-forward, stiffly listening. The sound had
come from behind her but she didn't turn. She remained still as
porcelain, looking into the eyes of her double seated opposite behind the pewter windowframes in an identical dim hotel room.
Even severely alert she couldn't help but smile at the reflection in
the checkerpaned french door. Silly sister, she said to herself and
her caged double smiled toothlessly back from the froth collar
of a flamingo pink dressing gown. A waterglass under a reflected
tablelamp fizzed with the grinning double's dentures and the
knees poking from the hem of the double's gown looked like the
skulls of two stillborn goats. Then she noticed the double's thin
hands had started roaming distractedly again over the pages of
the Bible open on the tight orlon lap. The smile went from the
double's face and the old woman forced herself to draw a long
slow breath until the nervous hands stilled, then she sighed aloud.

The sounds weren't doubled. From the other side of the pewter
bars came the spacious sound of a large city, late, lonely and vast
—nothing like the carpeted closeness of her hotel room with the
hum of plumbing and the sleeping child's breathing intimate

around her. She waited. The sound that had roused her from prayer had stopped, halted, to stand somewhere behind her, waiting at the end of the hall, if not at the door left where Keller-Brown shared a double with his wife, or at the right where the rest of the group enjoyed the suite, then waiting at hers, standing silently without knocking, pointedly without knocking. She did not move again until after many minutes when they turned and slowly left. Then she reached to the lamp and shut it off. "Silliness I swear." The sister image was replaced by a view of a tiny balcony with wrought-iron rail, and a thoroughfare two stories below empty under the streetlights.

By the tire-shined pavement and the prosperous business and storefronts she saw it was obviously a busy boulevard most of the time. The litter lying on the walks and in the gutters bespoke the usual activity: paper cups stabbed with straws in their lids; cigarette packs; fliers for massage parlors still fresh underfoot. . . . Now all was starkly still. Nothing moved except the light at the corner going from green to yellow to red and back to green; and that statue rotating. She squinted. It was some kind of mechanical advertisement, revolving relentless and spectral in the yards of one of the businesses across the street. As her eyes adjusted she tried to make out the features of the pirouetting effigy but her best guess still was that it resembled nothing so much as a cement moose holding a cement flying squirrel in his highlifted moose hand as he turned round and around and around. . .

"More silliness," she whispered to herself, absently; "Just more Los Angeles cra--"

As though a fingerprick from the dark pages had reminded her, she bent back to the book in her lap, as abruptly as she had been distracted from it—eyes clenched, hands roaming the invisible scripture and lips working again in a fervent resumption of her prayer:

*Let me be more specific about the kind of hand I'm advertising after: Somebody sharp, please, Lamb of God, someone sharp and shrewd and, alright, on the order of my Uncle Dicker to come right out and mention the beat of anybody I ever saw at uncloaking a flim-flam or smoking out a rat. Somebody—I guess I mean a hero as much as a helping hand, Lord—with not only the keen eye for detecting the cheat suspicioned but also the courage to call the rascal out. A hero. If no heroes are handy then leastways somebody to offer corroboration. Yes. Lena's Danial was a comfort to me in this respect; if it hadn't been for Danial checking into those lawyers Emery had hired in Little Rock against my instinctive suspicions I would've have been shystered out of what mineral rights I got left in the Bottom and would've had to get through these last twenty-five or so years with no income but that dadratted brown-tasting Welfare. So too did my grandson's wife, Betsy, stand me in similar stead, against them IRS weasels. In fact I guess there has been lots of similar helping hands through my journey now I think about it, but none of them represents the kernel of what I specifically mean right now like Uncle Dicker. It was his special-ty and his pride. It was what he was known for. "Dicker Topple can pick the paste from the pearls every time," it was said, and it was well known that not only couldn't nobody put one over on him personally but neither on anybody else if Uncle Dicker was on hand. It was his pride to the point of duty I guess, because I bet I personally seen him a hundred times step dutifully in at the last minute to steer Papa or Old Man Whittier or a relative or neigh-bor away from a bad horse trade by exposing some hostler's trick of horse or mule doctoring. It was the same with automobiles. When slick trading started turning from swayback animals and trick doctoring to brokedown machinery he was just as keen. He could detect chopped cork put in a gearbox just like he could pin-point a split hoof under a varnished coat of furniture putty. He told folks he had learned from a Mechanics Illustrated mail order course but, truth to tell, he never really knew that much about mechanics nor horseflesh neither. He could just naturally tell when somebody was pulling a fast one. This was how he came by his nickname, though I never saw him dicker after hardly a thing for himself; he'd just be there where the barter was happening, back out of the way a ways, leaned against a snubbing post or a gaspump while the dickering went on, whittling and yawning like he was bored by even the best bargains (in fact, he used to tell me that he never could get interested in good deals; that what really interested him was bad deals), nodding low-lidded over his kin-dlinstick so a stranger might easily assume him gone to the world unless something happened to lift his lids; then those glass-green eyes would douse down on some hornswaggle or hokeypokey like a waterwitcher's willow wand!*

*Dicker was Papa's older brother by a good many years—the oldest of the Topple brood and nearly as old as Emerson's daddy —and he had seen a lot of life far and near both as cabinboy on* one of the Confederate sidewheelers that ran rebel supplies up and down the Arkansas and the Ouchita rivers, then after the war as a fur trapper and after that as a traildriving cowboy and roust-about and all-around strongboy before he ruptured himself in a bet that he could lift a saddlepony with rider higher than his own six foot plus (he did it with a lift harness he rigged out of plow traces that went over his shoulders and down from a hayloft to the horse below saddled with full tack and straddled by the daring English-booted teenaged daughter of one of the ranchers he was betting against—giggling and gripping that saddlehorn between her legs while she kidded and teased and dared up at Uncle Dicker standing on the railroad ties spanning the haymow trapdoor over-head, ragging him while he heaved up a half a foot at a time with his back and legs then checked the traces with a pinch lever at his feet so's he could bend down and take in slack for another lift. The pony's hooves were just a hair shy of a two-yard hoe-handle off the barnᴠoor when Uncle Dicker busted a gut in two places. He said it wasn't the weight nor the pony's thrashing around in panic at being so high above the barnfloor but was that cussed sweet-faced rider getting up close enough to whisper to him that his trousers fly had popped open from the effort—a coy little whis-per so dripping with dare that he said he suspected right along it was nothing more than a fib to get his goat but by the time he'd bent to be sure it was too late) yet he never laid his shrewdness to his greater age or his more extensive experience. What he claimed he owed his knack of ungullibility to was—like his infirmity of the bowels—was to a girl, another sweetfaced, hairbrained prevari-cator from his cowdroving days or maybe even the same one. "Once you been good and skinned by a real Kansas City manskin-ner," he told folks, "there ain't nothing much these backcountry thimbleriggers can fleece off'n you," he often told folks how that skinning was what sparked the secret behind his shrewd ways but confided once to me that his secret was contained in a private phil-osophy that summed up says mainly Blessed Are They Who Ex-pect Nothing For They Shall Not Be Disappointed. "It ain't the hook that catches the fish, Becky, nor the fisherman. It's the fishes own open yap." Whichever, it was a talent that served him so re-liably for so many years that everybody'd pretty much give up the notion of ever seeing him seriously fooled—himself included —until the time we seen him get hooked at that family reunion. . .

This wasn't the last one in 1936 after Lena left home and Em-

*ery drove me back to Pine Bluff, but the next-to-the-last one ten years earlier and it was held at the Robroy Grange Hall in honor of Emerson's eldest sister, Old Man Whittier's only unmarried daughter Elvina (called for ages, I confess, "Whiney-Viney-Whittier Won't-some-fella-pity-her") being assigned a missionary post in some strange savage faraway place such as nobody would have been much surprised if she never returned from, nor disappointed either.*

*Most all four families come, not just for the possible last chance of seing Elvina but for, we knew, possibly the last chance of seeing a lot of us. Grandma Murphy, my grandmother from my mother's side, was crowding her century mark (a mark she never made; that winter was the big flu epidemic) and Emerson's father, Mr. Whittier, was nearing eighty as were lots of other relatives, aunts and uncles, grand-thises and great-thats, most of them pretty far down the road and showing it. Uncle Dicker was getting along himself but he looked pretty much like always, tall and strong and quiet, his hair cast iron gray and a slouchy limberness to the way he walked that was more ageless than old owing to a kind of graceful bobbing rhythm he had in his gait. When he walked he come clear up on his toes. When he was a little looped and was bobbing around this way, one palm pressed below his belt to hold in his hernia, he looked like a man dancing with a make-believe partner. And as he got more looped darned if he wouldn't get more graceful. In the Robroy Grange yard that afternoon with the hand not over his tummy hoisted high holding what must've been his fifteenth fruitjar of Papa's green homebrew he was so graceful, swaying amongst the relatives and the drizzling cottonwood and the plank tables piled with potluck, he looked like Fred Astaire waltzing merrily away. But never actually joining in any of the numbers with anybody until I coaxed him into being my partner for Oh Johnny saying A lady left lonely can't help but feel homely, Uncle Dicker, to which he retorts "She was only a dairyman's daughter but she was the cream of the crop," and swung me around so gay and exciting that remembering back it don't seem possible I was almost a grandmother myself and that longlegged lightfooted iron-steepled spire of a man was close to twice my age. What a switch from poor Emerson T. with his two left feet and both of them dangerous!*

*The music was loud and lively, furnished from the Grange's shady ivyhung front porch by a fiddle-and-guitar duet that Old*

*Man Whittier had seen perform at the Highlife Hotel in Shreve-
port at a cotton auction and had hired them for quite a fee to de-
viate from their tour to come and play for Viney's farewell frolic.
Everybody thought they was well worth the fee. They provided
us with real highlife sounds, though upon my honor both were
about as lowlifelooking a couple of troubadors as a fella might
ever flush from the gutter. Not so much the fiddler who was the
leader and whiteman of the two-toned ensemble—not at first, anyway. At first he seemed at worst your usual barbershop bigmouth
approaching flashy-trashy in checkered pants striped suspenders
and polkadotted bowtie with customary long sideburns and big
mustache, and a face almost handsome but for that outsized red-
lipped mouth he couldn't quite keep puckered from sight under
that mustache. . . just your usual fiddler dandy you might've
thought if you'd seen him alone and without his partner and accompanist on the guitar who was an unusually horrid sight. He
was a Choctaw Indian, full-blooded and filthy and terribly gouged
with the pox as were most of what was left of the South's red race.
He played the guitar well enough but with such a puss to behold
a listener might never notice the music. In addition to the effect of
this complexion and the cloud of flies who were doubtless fans of
his filthy aroma, the Indian was festooned with every sort of pagan accoutrement imaginable, from rabbits' feet by the dozens, to
glassbead strings by the yards, to two little gopher skulls dangling
from his big hairy earlobes. And he was humpbacked, crook-
necked and blind. Not shut-eye blind, either; popeye blind! Both
balls stuck right out there like eggs half-poached. A sightless
sight, sure enough!*

*Prudently, the fiddler kept him playing his guitar back in the
shadows of the porch as much as he could and did the talking for
the two of them. I say prudently but, as the afternoon fiddled and
the beer flowed on and on, he got to talking too much even for two.
And he talked in a sort of accent that wandered back and forth
between France and Dixie so there was a taunting phoniness to
his talking that was downright brazen, and it got brassier as he
got boozier until it became practically a slap in your face. It really began to gall as the shadows got long. Especially on Uncle
Dicker and especially when Mr. Foucart Dulcet, as he called himself, got to hoorawing the kids and young girls about the Indian,
who they were naturally fascinated by: "Shoo now, children, mon
littlepetites; shoo!" he would warn a cluster creeping close to*

*gawk at the smelly apparition humped over his guitar in the scup-*
*pernong shadows; "Was I you I'd pay attention. I am your friend*
*as well as hired fiddle. I give you wise council. And believe me I*
*dislike having to bring a dark note to this bright occasion but was*
*I you-all I would not pester Hush-As-Death." Then roll his eyes,*
*more taunting them on than shooing them back. "Yes, for that is*
*his monicker, children: Hush. As. Death. A bonafide medicine*
*man from your wild land, a natural born 'shee-law' of supernat-*
*ural powers, powers mighty and mysterious beyond our Christian*
*ken, children, and not! to be trifled with! Stay back I warn you-*
*all. He can conjure spirits. He can call out the crick witches if he's*
*trifled with, to fill your sleep with dreams of burning to death or*
*drowning under the ice in a froze-over river. Look out—!" Then*
*wink at the menfolk or leer wickedly at the maids and let his lips*
*spread into a laugh that got redder and less funny with every beer*
*"—he's swaying and humming! Yes, he's doing his hatchet hex!*
*Was I you children I would fear for my privates. EEhah!"*

*Everybody was getting tired of it; in its own way the laugh*
*coming out of that big red mouth like gore itself was as nasty a*
*business as the Indian's looks.*

*"If it weren't for that fiddler fellas ears," Uncle Dicker finally*
*had to remark outloud after one such grizzly display; "the whole*
*top of his greasy head would come off in a island everytime he*
*grins." Outloud enough I saw the fiddler redden and snap the lips*
*back under the mustache like some obscene rubber device that had*
*slipped into view. Uncle Dicker had hit his tender spot and he*
*kept it tucked in a pout out of sight the rest of the afternoon and*
*stuck to the music and layed off the beer like he'd been scolded*
*tame. But his eyes were into Uncle Dicker's back, I noticed, every-*
*time it was turned.*

*Twilight brought the chill up out of the Bottom and we moved*
*from the yard into the low-ceilinged lamplit grange hall. The*
*women did the dishes and palletted down the kids while the men*
*worked on that keg and thumb wrestled and pitched pennies, and*
*then dimes then quarters till they finally got out the poker cards.*
*Then Mr. Dulcet traded his fiddle for a long black stogie and*
*commenced to grin again. He eyed those cards like some sharp-*
*shooters at a turkey shoot eye a gun being loaded. I thought sure*
*he was going to have a go at Uncle Dicker, the way they'd been*
*circling each other, but he didn't sit in at the game at all. He never*
*even lit the cigar. He just pulled the stool close and sat there with*

*it stuck cold in his grin—a silent spectator.*

*His partner wasn't behaving so good, though. Squatted on a
bench by the Grangehall wall the Indian was finishing his third
plate of potato salad and was beginning to rock and make a kind
of nasty humming mumble in his throat. Everybody got more and
more peeved but tried not to mention it. The game went on. The
humming got louder and louder until finally the Indian thrust his
empty plate out into the lamplight and demanded fourths with a
loud "Huh! Hoo! Huh!" and Elvina sang out from the kitchen
Don't that pagan talk? and Mr. Dulcet took his cigar out of his
mouth and said that we might not fathom the language, but talk
he surely did; how else did we think he caught all them rabbits?
Rabbits? we say. For the feet, he says, "Bereft of the blessing of
sight, Hush had to talk them into his clutches. He charmed them,
with a Choctah spell wove as thick and slick as the handwove net
he used. I was privy to the sight of him doing it and I tell you it
was something terrible!" So pompous does he say this that Uncle
Dicker had to smart back Anybody can trap swamp rabbits even
blind heathens, and Mr. Dulcet says: "O no! No, these aren't ordinary these rabbits he catches; for the foot to have power its got
to come from the left front leg of a midnightcaught Graveyard rab-
bit!" then went cherrily into that old kid's rhyme keeping time
with his stogies*

> *Over the carven slab he goes*
> *His nest is hid from the human eye;*
> *Every root in the night he knows*
> *And he 'ludes the trappers every try.*
>
> *But the charm words spoke on the midnight air*
> *Can coax him out from beneath his root;*
> *There's a fortune for whoever lays the snare*
> *And whoever severs his furry foot.*

*It was still when he finished. The plate of food came. The kero-
sene flickered and the shadows danced and the Indian rocked and
mumbled over his food. That is pretty thick stuff all right, Elvina
says, impressed in spite of herself, and Uncle Dicker says It don't
matter if you slice it thick or if you slice it thin, it's still baloney.
Everybody laughed and Mr. Dulcet drew in his grin and looked
around hurt. "You doubt, is that it? Which? My word or Hush's*

*powers? Or is it both? Yes, I see it's both. Very well. I make no conjecture why you doubt me—who can guess what mystery causes a civilized fellow to mistrust without just cause whatsoever his civilized brother?—but I have to say, folks, your reason for mistrusting Hush is nothing mysterious. I understand you folks."* He was starting to sound a little more Yankee than Dixie. *"I understand you there, by golly. You mistrust him because he's different. You doubt him because he's a blind heathen not of the caucasian race and none too pretty to boot. Understandable; completely understandable."* He shook his head like a New York liberal saddened deeply by such a heartless world, but again his voice was more taunting than sad: *"Grown folks, civilized folks, laughing at the less fortunate. But say. I'll teach you-all a lesson. I'll dare you to a showdown on this, by golly! I will wager, in all seriousness, wager that poor blind Hush can see in some ways a lot better than you civilized cardsharpies laughing at him."* And pulled from his vest pocket a roll of greenbacks big as a flashlight battery and unrolled it amongst the nickels and dimes and matchsticks.

*Now he had everybody's attention sure enough. He said he proposed a test, a scientific experiment to demonstrate Hush-As-Death's powers of second sight and that he would cover any bet large or small of anybody with the stomach for it. He bet we could shuffle that deck and cut it and the Indian could find the card cut to "without aid of natural forces." "We shuffle?" Uncle Dicker asks. "You shuffle." "We cut?" Uncle Dicker asks and Mr. Dulcet says "You cut, Mr. Topple. Nor never let me see the card. You got the stomach for it?" Uncle Dicker set a long time thinking about it while everybody waited. Then he laid out a ten-dollar bill and the rest of the men started digging for their hips. Mr. Dulcet covered them all, grinning around the stogie. The kids came sneaking up from their pallets and the wives edged out of the kitchen to watch. Papa shuffled the deck then Dwight Murphy shuffled it a second time, then slid it to Uncle Dicker. He cracked his knuckles and cut up a red three. He showed it around, careful to keep it turned from Mr. Dulcet on his stool. "Now right back where it come from, Mr. Dicker," Mr. Dulcet said. "Home to beddy-bye."—and tapped the half deck on the table. "You gonna reshuffle?" Uncle Dicker wanted to know but Mr. Dulcet laughed and drew back with his cheroot held high. "These hands haven't touched these documents yet, have they? I'd be a fool to leave a* opening for suspicions now, wouldn't I?" Uncle Dicker returned the cut and squared the deck, his eyes on the mouth stretching out across the chalky face. "Call him," Mr. Dulcet whispered. "What?" "Over to find the card. Call him!" "What the hell do I call him?" Uncle Dicker was whispering too. "Call him Hush-As-Death and ask him to find your card." Uncle Dicker cleared his throat a time or two and finally called "Hush! Hay! you Hush. Come over here. We want, would like for you to. . ."

The Indian was down off the bench and scuffing toward the table, arms outstretched and white eyes shining. He halted when his knick-knack-laden leather pantslegs bumped into the table edge. He felt around till he found the deck then spread it in a sweep across the tabletop and, without any fanfare or fuss at all, flipped the red three face-up in the light, turned and scuffed straight back to his plate by the wall and finished the potato salad in silence.

Mr. Dulcet climbed at last from the stool and intoned to the bigeyed kids, "So you see, children; it is as I told you: Powerful —" he carefully put the deck of cards back in neat order then started stacking the pile of bills. "Powerful and deep the medicine of this ancient people. Not to be trifled with." He rolled his winnings into a cylinder twice the size it had been, returned it to his vest pocket. He took up his fiddle case and, lending an arm to his belching associate, walked out of the hall into the still evening leaving Uncle Dicker staring at the deck, slackjawed and befuddled, the skin of his face beginning at last to show the beers. Show the beers and the years. And when I saw him again at Lena and Danial's wedding it just about broke my heart; only about four years had gone by but my hero uncle was fuddlebit to the point of infirmity. He was nervous and uncertain in his movements and avoided meeting my look when we talked. And his face was still blanched. I knew it was that fiddler's sucker-rod still sunk into Uncle Dicker's heart and I wondered if he'd even last the year at the rate his color was being sucked off. There wasn't any hue left at all except I could still see that red three in his face: It looked more painful than three hernias and just as permanent.

So when we headed back that last time in '36 I was fearfully anxious for how he'd stood up. I didn't know that I could stand seeing him completely broke down and the closer we got the more the prospect haunted me. I was about to ask Emerson to drive on to town and let's rest up a night in the hotel first but before I could

137

*think of a way to say it we were at the gate and there he was com-
ing across the yard to our car stepping, for all my fret, high and
full of vinegar as ever. His hair was a little whiter, maybe, but not
his face. The sunny color had come back to his cheeks completely,
and I thought how glorious are the ways of God that everything
can be mended. Like a smart old wolf Uncle Dicker had crawled
off to lick his wounds healed and forget his aches, to let time do
its wonder. "Healed" I thought to myself. It wasn't till we drove
into Pine Bluff the next day to the Moose Lodge where we were
having this one that I seen he hadn't healed at all. He wasn't even
bad hurt. "He just wasn't done," I said to myself the instant I seen
the man on the stage with his mustache prickling and his chin
clamped cocky on his fiddle as he bowed a merry hoedown.*

*I just had to sit down and gawk at him, tapping his toe and wink-
ing his flirt at the girls, innocent as a lamb that this reunion was
anything other than a hundred other such small town to-dos he'd
fiddled at before. He'd acquired a little Van Dyke to go with his
handlebars. He sported a bigger diamond ring. And the clothes
he had on were gone past merely flashytrashy and was headed
for elegant—butteryellow shoes and necktie; the very latest in
nonshrink nor wrinkle slacks and sport coat cut from some of the
new synthetic miracle material that flashed blue when it creased
one direction and peagreen purple the other; even a soft burgundy
fedora with a band of that same modern material. And stuck in
the band like a feather, a black cheroot, just like the other right
down to him never lighting only using it between numbers to chew
on or wave around while he jabbered his jokes and baloney (I
think by sucking on the cold butt he reminded his renegade mouth
to stay under his mustache). He had traded in his European accept on a second-hand Will Rogers twang and now billed himself
on the posterboard tacked to the Master Moose's podium as "Harry Cheery Old Favorites in New Wrappings & Accompaniment.
Requests Welcomed." but there was no mistaking it was Mr.
Dulcet.*

*"What did you say Becky sweetheart?" Uncle Dicker finally
asks. "Nary a word," I say. "Is that a fiddler or not?" he further
asks, very loud, though I was right next to him: "Cost twohundred
dollars plus trainfare to get him out here from California but he's
worth every cent, ain't he? Ain't he everybody? Not only can he
fiddle he comes dressed out like a rich preacher in rut." By the
laugh from the menfolks I seen nearly everybody but the fiddler*

*was in on it. "Say Mr. Cheery" Uncle Dicker calls, "what do you think of our fair state? Ever passed through this neck of the woods before?" "In Song only" the fiddler shot back and bowed a few licks of Arkansas Traveller; "How about you? Ever out to Caly-foreigny?"*

*"Only once, through Susanville after muscrats for a couple of weeks," Uncle Dicker says; "But trappin was nothin but slow."*

*Mr. Dulcet noticed a loose horse hair on his bow; he returned the stogie to his hatband and reached inside his coat for a knife, clicked it open and sliced off the stray. "The whole burg is nothing but slow," he says; folding the blade shut against his leg and returning it to his bosom. "I spent a couple weeks there one day myself is how slow." And haw-hawed into the next number.*

*Back under the moosehead set his new accompanist, awfuller if possible than the last, a fat mariachi Mexican in silverstudded black naugahyde cartridge belts crossing his bloated belly and in his naugahyde holsters two pearl-handled kid cap pistols. Jeweled rings fairly dripping off his fat fingers and as you looked close you saw his hands, from his knuckles up his puffy wrists clean into his lacy cuffs, was tatooed with crosses and skulls and little dingy words that made me thankful I couldn't read Mexican. His face was ruint just like his predecessor's had been and then some. Instead of pox it was scars, a regular pattern of scars not deep but deliberate like crisscrosses sliced in a doughball that rose to a loaf then was baconfat glazed and overbaked. And, also like old Hush, blind. Not bugeye blind but worse. No-eye blind, and with sanitary napkin wads that looked like they hadn't been changed in a month. I also noted that in a scabbard built into his fancy black boots was a pearlhandled slicer I bet was no kids' toy. "You sure you're in the right stirring up this old argument?" I whispered. Uncle Dicker grinned and whispered back, "Darlin' Becky, when the rooster argues with the cockroach the rooster is allus in the right."*

*With everybody acquainted with their parts in this rerun except the musicians it wasn't no trouble maneuvering them into position. It went the same, darned near to the Mexican's rude grunt for refills only this time I took Elvina's part and Danial shuffled because Papa was getting arthritis. Even the unlit black stogie conducted the shuffling and the bet like it had to be the same. Like when Uncle Dicker only put down a five some of our folks hesitated, wavering, until Uncle Dicker reassured them by adding a*

139

*second. Then here come the greenbacks, so thick and fast it made the fiddler's eyes narrow; "Say I'll give you sports in this neck of the woods one thing by god," he said, sucking at his liphair; "Country, you may be but penny ante you ain't."*

*Uncle Dicker made like to pick the money back up sighing well if this is too rich for Caly-forignee. . . But the fiddler said no no no I stand behind my man (he called this one Hombre Powerful, and had warned the kids if they provoked him he would make a voodoo model of their bedrooms and by squinting one of the cotton wads at the dollhouse window could see what they were doing any hour of the night til they was asleep, married or dead) and dug into his inside jacket pocket for more cash.*

*The card was a red jack and as soon as it was directed back into the deck he had us call his "Power Man." The pusslegutted Mexican stood right up and thumped right over and found it as easy as he could have located one of the doorknob diamonds on his fingers. Everybody was flabbergasted: "Dicker damn you" Papa spluttered as he watched his ten gathered in with the rest of the stakes. "— I thought you claimed, meant, —" "I never meant he couldn't locate the card agin," Uncle Dicker said. "Then what in hell damn did you mean?" "That he couldn't get away with it agin," he said and like a limber snake striking had that cigar out of that mouth ". . . is all I meant." He snapped it between his fingers and poured onto the table over the deck and amongst the change and matchsticks a good tablespoon of white crystals. "What is it?" Papa asked. "Salt," Uncle Dicker crowed. "Salted the cut with this trickstore cigar. The salt acks like little ballbearings so's the deck —" Mr. Harry Dulcet Cheery sprang back from the circle, digging again at the inside of the double-color sportscoat but Danial had him by the shoulders before he could get the knife open. He hollored something in Spanish and the Mexican drug out his knife and sliced the wind a couple of vicious ones before Papa knocked him down from behind with the Moose's longhandled collection pot and confiscated his dagger. He shook his head and jumped back up with another pigsticker produced from his sleeve and Papa got him again. Everytime the Mexican would come around he would out with another blade and start swinging blind until Papa bopped him with the longhandled pot and relieved him of his weapon. I could hear one of the women already on the telephone to the authorities while we tied up the fiddler with his own butterbright necktie. We could have tied the accom-*

plice but Papa was enjoying himself thoroughly, circling the cussing drunken Mexican who was now down to a boyscout knife.

The fiddler was screeching a mile a minute while they tied up his hands—begging, threatening, insulting us one second and appealing to our Christian mercy the next. Finally Uncle Dicker reached over and jerked off one whole half his mustache. The blood oozed out and he kept licking it off and sputtering but he didn't say no more for fear of the other half.

"What about his shill, Dicker. Haul him in, too?" Papa asked. Dicker looked him over and says Naw, let him go. "How come? You figure being blind and Mexican is penalty enough?"

"That ain't; no," Uncle Dicker said: "Shilling for a skunk like this is, though. I doubt blind people ever have much trouble getting into the Promised Land, even Mexicans, but shilling for a skunk like this marks a man so's he can't be sure of a welcome anyplace. That's penalty enough."

So they turned the Mexican loose and the one-handled fiddler over to the constables. Apparently, though, he never done any jail time. Cousin Maggie Murphy wrote me that by the time the trial come up on the calendar Dicker the prosecution's prime witness had lost enthusiasm or track or maybe finally just lost interest again now that he'd settled the slate. Anyway he never could be found to testify the day of the hearing so the skunk was acquitted. Uncle Dicker passed on, they wrote, not many months after the trial. He wasn't ailing, they wrote, he just cashed it in one afternoon, on the old Topple Place front porch in his whitepine shavings. They buried him in the Confederate cemetery in Jefferson County, Arkansas, and they had inscribed on his stone, or so they wrote us, the epitaph: "HERE LIES RICHARD 'DICKER' TOPPLE A WIDEAWAKE MAN ASLEEP AT LAST" which I plan to visit when I'm back there to add underneath But Don't Let This Tempt You Into Trying Nothing Fast

They came again. This time she turned her head, squinting over her shoulder across her darkened room. She could make out the outline of the door pencilled from the black by the hall light outside. They hadn't been loud, barely discernable above the tinny, premorning roar of the city. She knew they weren't loud enough to attract any notice from any of the other guests on the floor; they reached her ears only because they were addressed so.

This time she could see them; they interrupted the stripe of light at the bottom of the door and waited there, knockless. She watched, her neck twisted sharply, fingers of one hand moving over the page of the open Bible. The shadow turned and the footsteps retreated down the hall. She twisted back around and licked the fingers that had been tracing the dark page. She scowled at the taste, as though the paper, print, the passage itself had become stinging to the tongue. Then moved the fingers down between the buttons of her dressing gown to a large welt on her stomach. That's what comes of asking for signs! she thought as she caressed the sting. The very asking for signs, it seemed like, had volunteered both mortal flesh and the immortal pages of faith into the territory of stinging! Ouch! When I shut the kitty in the drawer and doped myself to sleep in the old Nebo cabin twenty-four hours earlier I had thought, Lord, if You mean me to volunteer for this mission probably the first thing You'll give me won't be neither the certainty I'm asking for nor the strength but just some little signal that I ought to rise up in time, and, sure as shooting, right as the sun was breaking through the mist in the cottonwoods, a derned old dirtrobber stung me right in the belly. I rose up then sure enough! I sprang from that bed like a fish breaking water and sung out Glory yes Lord I discern the face of the sky *and* the signs of the times! Referring, of course, to Matthew sixteen three because the nasty things were *every*where. Evidently the heater had warmed up the cabin to incubation temperature. Early in the year as it was they were hatching out of the cracks by the scads. I put on my sidezipper slacks and my white silk top from Oriental Imports while I said my morning vespers all in a nervous hurry and asked at the end, "Whatever happened to Gabriel and his horn incidentally, Lord? Or a plain old rooster?" as I kept swatting away with my slipper.

By the time I was packed and hurrying up the frostly old board walk the welt on my tummy was the size and complexion of a red Mexican chilipepper, and ten times as hot. I checked in my compact and my eyes were the same fiery hue, indicating clearly I could've used more than two hours rest if you can call it that. Still and all, I felt as fired-up as if I'd drunk a gallon of hot black coffee in my sleep. Usually just one of them pills knocks me out for dern near the whole next day, and leaves me dim and soggy as a campfire after a cloudburst even days later. But whatever had lit me up so last night at the party had kept smouldering through *three* of them like they wasn't but a sprinkle. Then that mud wasp under the covers had fanned it all aflame.

I bustled right along. I could hear motors running. Coming around the corner of the barn I see Mr. Keller-Brown had already drove his bus up from the ash grove and roused the other two Birds of Prayer vehicles: a van and another bus. Both of which were showing a lot more mileage than the Keller-Brown luxury liner but were nevertheless in good condition, painted nice new white over their old bodies with that flying cross of five purple bird-designs that was the band's trademark. All three were nosed in toward the middle of the lot where all the cars had been parked yesterday. From their rearends they were sporting big plumes of exhaust in the morning nip and in the area before their grills the menfolk stood in a circle talking; there was my two grandsons, and that muddlehead Claude, and the big-bearded black fellow who played the guitar for the band, and Mr. Keller-Brown. They were all wrapped in blankets or coats and stamping from foot to foot the way men do, whether it's chilly or not, when they are waiting on women. I slowed down and caught my wind. I couldn't hear them over the engines but I could read the serious little smoke signals of their conversation enough to bet they were discussing last night's events. They didn't notice me till I was right on top of them and sung out Say, if this here show is going to make it to the Hollywood Bowl tomorrow sunup we better get it on the road!

You could've knocked them off their feet with a feather! Especially my grandson Devlin. He says you must be kidding and I says not unless Mr. Keller-Brown was when he invited me. Keller-Brown was combing out the burrs of the evening with his fancy ivory arrow quills at the back making a comb. He assures me he was most assuredly *not* kidding—sticking that arrow in his hair so he can take my hand in both his—and that he would be *deeply honored*. He squeezed my hand and gave me a secret grateful relieved look for my not mentioning the scolding he give me in the ash grove. I couldn't help but sqeeze back. And Devlin says of course anybody would be honored but that there's been some changes since that offer: "M'kehla has picked up some new problems since yesterday, Grandma; and a new passenger." I say well if there isn't room of course. Mr. Keller-Brown says it isn't that: there's still plenty of room: "It's only his, the con*dition of* this new passenger, Mrs. Whittier. . ." Everybody snuffed and looked down at the dew a moment, waiting on each other. Buddy finally explains "He's got Otis Kone in there Grandma. Kind of crazy." I tell them what of it, "I stood up under his craziness before, ain't

I?" Buddy says this wasn't Otis' customary craziness: "After you left the party last night Otis' craziness got very real!" Keller-Brown says "We had to finally sedate him." "Sedate the hell out of him," Claude Muddle adds. They were still again. I says well the more the better, and ask "What was it? You figured you had to sedate him to get him to hold still long enough so's you can cart him back south where crazies are more at home, is that it?" Keller-Brown grins and says So he can see his own analyst. I say all the better, "A fellow ought to see his own doctor in his own hometown. Just show me what sedation you're using and I'll make sure he doesn't suffer till he gets there." They were still again. Claude Muddle shook his head; "Granny, you are either an even better Samarian than I thought or you want to go to California more than I ever imagined." I correct him that's Samaritan, Claude Muddle, then tell them all "And the only person that I'm really thinking about is my own selfish self. Not only do I get my life-long wish of attending a Sunrise Service at the Hollywood Bowl, I *also* can get to that mineral rights business you boys have been trying to get me to attend to. Well, I never flew but once, and that was before the invention of the airplane. And to a place so beyond Pine Bluff that I was spoiled and do not aim to repeat the experience until I can sail the same way to the same place. And if I heard right, if Mr. Keller-Brown and *you*-all —" I said this at the big-bearded fellow because he hadn't spoke his piece on my sudden attachment to their troup. "— are a-movin' east right after Los Angeles —" "Us-all? A-movin'?" That's what I'm asking, yes." The beard bloomed into a grand grin, "Why *ma'am*, right after. To Vegas, Santa Fe, Oklahoma City is mighty pretty." A look to Mr. Keller-Brown nipped the grin before it could blossom into a laugh: "Then right on to Little Rock. . . a-movin'!" I say I thought so and in as I am not going to fly and never had a easier motorride than in that fancy bus and bed that if Mr. Keller-Brown and you all can put up with an old fool clean back to Arkansas I can surely put up with a fat sedated one down to southern California. Devlin opened his mouth to protest further but just then his front door banged open across the lot and out come the women, two of the colored singers carrying an ice chest between them followed by Mrs. Keller-Brown hugging a big bundle of freshfolded laundry and chatting with Betsy Deboree. Betsy'd put on a plain jacket over her nightdress and had a big brown lunchbag under one arm and the child by the hand at the end of the other as

she helped him, almost extra-carefully as is Betsy's very convincing levelheaded way, down the frosty frontporch steps. He seen
me before the women did. I saw him see me before he got halfway
down the steps, but—obedient little angel that he is—didn't pull
loose till he got to the gravel at the bottom. Then he come a-scoot-
in, across the lot through the litter of coke cups and religious fliers
like a streak, without grin nor greeting, till he was at my side tug-
ging my arm up and down like it was the bellrope to my heart.
"Besides," I told the menfolk; "I sorta promised a feller." After
that even levelheaded Betsy couldn't have convinced me different.

They had Otis in a skyblue mummy bag, zippered to the chin
and stretched out on the recline-o-lounger. Across the chest and
on around the tipped back of the chair they'd tied the big American flag to make sure he wasn't going anywhere. Not that he
looked neither inclined or capable. The face showing out of the
puckered Orlon hole was both tight-swollen—from sunburn, and
chickenwire, and Lord knows what other mortifications—yet still
slack from the sedation. A bloody drool ran out of the corner of
his limp mouth and tears out of the corners of his eyes. His eyes
was partly open, even kind of awake, but there was no more con-
scious consciousness in them than in two sticky old jawbreakers.
I could see the only problem we were likely to have with this patient was keeping the flag tight so he wouldn't go slopping out of
the recline-o-lounger around the corners.

Claude Muddle had scrounged a real stethoscope out of his own
bus and presented it to Toby, and I had pinned on one of Otis'
pamphlets blankside out in my hair. We had clinic. Before we was
ten miles south of Nebo the little doctor with his big solemn serious learned gaze and his dedicated old nurse had the situation well
in hand. After a good warm face-wash and a check of the pulse in
the neck we decleared Otis' condition stable and took up vigil on
the cushions beside the recline-o-lounger. Between tall tales and
Betsy's jellied snaps we administered to our patient. I would wet-
wipe his nose and eyes and mouth when necessary, and Toby
would then check for signs of a relapse. With his stethoscope he
would listen to the chin, the cheeks, mostly the forehead because
that was where his father had told him Otis' problem come from
—"A mind gone decayed and dent." I told him I concurred, careful not to laugh at his pronounciation. Old as I was I remembered
the main rules of playing doctor: the nurse is never as smart.

The bus hummed. We played doctor. And as the miles rolled

away, so did the years. The only thing that kept the game from being completely fun was the eyes of the patient. After while I talked Toby into borrowing a pair of his daddy's sunglasses from the assortment Mr. Keller-Brown had lined up along his dashboard, but they weren't completely successful. They were the big wraparound mirror lenses and made Otis look like some kind of deceased rocketship pilot in his shiny blue suit and red rocketship chair draped with the stars and stripes . . . the corpse of an American astronaut hero decked out for a burial in space.

We kyoodled right along to the tune of flutes and lutes and tootles from every sort of creed or country. Mr. Keller-Brown could reach back from the driver's seat to a bank of knobs and, without taking his eye off the road, switch us from a Catholic men's chorus singing Latin from the dark ages to darkest Africa with converted natives chanting the very same thing. I hadn't hardly said diddledy squat to him since we left. There wasn't really anyplace for me to sit up by the driver, and he had the earphones on most of the time. Besides I knew there was nothing either of us had to say to each other as pressing as the questions we wouldn't be. For all my performance this morning he couldn't help but be wondering why I'd come along after last night, and for all the dead kitty and the wasp to wake me I feared I couldn't speak but be asking, not in so many actual words but nevertheless as obvious as the growling belly of a bear, Are you really as evil as I thought in the spooky night, really such a threat as needs have me along to protect innocent flesh? Or are you just a uppitty fella and me just an old bored busybody looking for an excuse to play doctor?

Behind us come the three ladies in the second bus driven by the big-bearded fellow who clowned around and made faces at Toby and we when he saw us looking out the rearwindow. Behind this come the van with all the drums and guitars and loudspeaker machinery and so forth. Driving this was a little old fella knotty and brown and bitter as a twist of chewing tobacco that Toby said went by the name of Background and used to work for Duke Ellington and Lena Horne and a *long time ago*, he tells me, his big blue eyes getting respectfully bigger, "I remember he worked for the *Great Louis Armstrong!*" Great and *late* I tell him. "Louis Armstrong was dead and buried before you was hatched, honeylamb. He says "No . . . No because I got the autograph he gave me." The little fella went forward to his desk and come back with a book full of pictures of famous and not-so-famous Negro musicians which he leafed through till he found the particular photo and read "To Toby a double-hip cat from his main man Louis" and gave me a look, not the slightest I-told-you-so but respectful and resigned (even if somewhat nose-wrinkled) and forgiving, as to say "I can't blame you for doubting my word because I myself find it hard to believe me a mere child knew such great men. But here's the proof. . . ."

He leafed on through the pictures and read them off to me, as if it was a family album: Who they were, what they did, their honors and titles. All were signed with different inscriptions and signatures—To Toby with affection from the Count . . . To Lover Toby from Queen of the Blues . . . To October Brown from Brother James—but all in what looked to me like the same pen and in the same hand give or take a few curlicues. He dribbled silent before he finished then shut it and sat looking at an old spill stain on the fancy leather cover. "It's a real nice book," I told him and ask who give it to him, his daddy? He said no it wasn't his daddy he didn't think. "Ol' Backdrop then? He looks like the jazzy sort . . . " He said no, he thought it must have been his Uncle Ronald because his picture was the last and biggest in the book. He opened it up again to a fullpage glossy portrait of the big-bearded fellow up on a smoky little cramped stage. He was with a different band altogether, and he was the drummer (stick type), his face fairly afire with the delight he felt pounding away in the spotlight behind those shiny affairs. You could see drops of sweat flying off him twenty feet around. "Besides, there's another one Background gave me."

It was the twin of the first scrapbook to the stains on the leather, and the pictures inside looked like they'd been pasted in in just about the number of hours it would take for a couple of fellows to finish off a quart of hootch and a pint of mucilage. But not many of this new collection was even real photos. Most had been snipped from boxing magazines or Negro pin-up publications. More often than not they weren't signed so much as scrawled over in pencil with bits and snatches like "I got no fight with them Viet-Kong—M. Ally" and "De Good Lawd says Dat's good—J. Johnson" and "I am black but O my soul is white—W. Blake."—Some of them with some pretty hard words and all of them with some increasingly boozey penmanship, but I be switched if he wasn't reading them all aloud! Stiff and slow, a little uncertain because a lot of the quotes must not've made no sense to him (nor me, nor anybody, I suspected) but letter perfect he read them! I ask him to tell me again how old he is. He says four years four months and some days. "Just four and a *half years old!?*" Now it was my eyes turn to go wide and no fooling. "Four and a half not even in first grade and already *reading*? Reading *writing*? You fibber you must be *twicet* that. Look me in the eye . . . " Four and a half he repeated, unblinking and unflattered. All I could do was roll my eyes. It was beginning to dawn on me why all this fuss was always made over him. I had assumed he was reciting them autographs out of the other book by memory, the way a youngster can after he gets somebody to read him a favorite tale over enough times, but there wasn't any way anybody could've memorized this pencilied silliness even if it was their favorite. One thing didn't follow another.

"I can even read Bible writing," he said, again without any trace of boast or brag save perhaps it was in the awe I began to sense he held himself in. I says Bible writing? Your daddy must be as good a teacher as he is a seamstress. Or is it your mother? He says all of them was his teachers. Before she'd moved into the other bus he said he'd been learning to read arithmetic because she wanted him to be a scientist when he grows up. And Uncle Ronald was teaching him to read music, he told me. This subject perked him up a lot more than the subject of arithmetic. "Uncle Ronald and Background say I got The Natural. They both say I could grow up the True New Bird!" I says was the Old Bird another jazz Late and Great? "Greater than anybody," he says, touching my arm. He looked up into my face, intimate and enthusiastic: "I can play all of *How Long* on Chastity's lady guitar and almost all of *Nobody Knows You* except for the F's. I can't reach the F's yet. My fingers aren't long enough . . . " He dribbled to a stop again and took his hand off. He shut the book and stared at a place out past the top of it. He says he knows he could get it, eventually, but he doesn't really think it's what he wants to be anyway. When he grows up . . . The greatest musician in America . . . Doesn't think it's what his father wants, either. I ask "What's he got in mind, honey? President of the United States?" He shakes his head No, not President . . . his father says by the time he gets growed-up there won't be any more president or United States or *any* states . . . that the whole world will be one big happy congregation. I tell him that's a pleasant prospect and ask if there's any predictions when it's due because I'd hate to miss it. But he isn't listening anymore. He's watching out the window with that expression on his face not so much wrinkled by distaste for what he might see out there in the blue yonder as with indignation over having to look in any yonder at all . . . like a pious puritan farmer might look were he compelled to watch a neighbor's color TV because he needed to know what the weather satellite had to say about tomorrow's haying prospects. "And I think he wants me to be the Preacher of it, because it's him has me read out of the Bible, my Father. That's the hardest for me to get, Bible writing . . . Like the F . . . " He yawned, watching the passing slashes of mountaintop and sky. "But sometimes, when he has me start in just where I open it and doesn't stop me to explain, I do get it. The words come out like they're my own and I think 'Maybe I am . . . ' " Then puts aside the scrapbook and lays back, still yawning. He hadn't taken his eyes from the window. He tried a time or two to tug the cotton pullover down over the slice of his tummy showing, then gave up and folded his hands over the bare strip. I swear he was cute, as sweet and dimply a little sugarlump as ever fingered a bellybutton. But for that nose-wrinkled look. "Am what?" I asked him after a bit and he says "Pardon me?" "Sometimes you think maybe you maybe am what?" "Going to be." "Going to be what?" "Be the Preacher. If I keep studying and learning, and grow up . . . Well, I'm going to go to sleep now, Grandma," he says, dismissing me. Though it was miles before he turned from the window and closed eye one.

After the child dozed off I moseyed up the carpeted bus to chin with Mr. Keller-Brown. He was as polite as pie. He took off his earphones and reached me a folding campstool to sit on. He said again how glad he was I'd joined on. He told me he'd been watching the two of us back there and hadn't seen Toby so Happy in months. "I am grateful, Mrs. Whittier. More than grateful. And more than ashamed for my freakout last night. *Mm!* Damn me, I don't know. I get paranoid about him, I guess . . . overprotective . . . and overwrought and overinvolved and over hot-headed dumb nigger, I guess. Damn me!" There was a raw edge to his words that was a little scary. I told him after riding these hours alone with the little pup I could see why he was overprotective. "He is a gem and a rare one," I says, and that any parents would be overprotective with him. He adjusted the mirror into my face and after a long look, he reached back and turned the sound

149

down and says "Mrs. Whittier, my lady Lev and I, as you probably picked up on, are into a thing. I mean for the last few months
she and I, we haven't been exactly copascetic, y'know? We'll work
it out but—I mean we *are* working it out but, like always, it's the
kid bruised in the workout. So, to be frank, I could use some —"
He saw me watching his face in the mirror and got so embarrassed
he went abruptly into his darky act. "Ah *means*, Miz Whittier,
whatever you got to offer my lil boy, go *rat ahead on!*" What he
was saying was that any more cameos or cats that this old white
angel might be inclined to give in the future was okay with this
darky. A blackfolks Seal of Goodhousekeeping Approval he was
awarding me . . .

I began to feel a little sorry for Mr. Keller-Brown. He seemed
so insulated and cut off from folks, the way a fella will get sometimes after sustaining a real bad hurt, or bad beating or robbery
or fuss, something bad enough that he'd mortgaged everything
long ago for secret weapons and electric alarms to ward off any
approach, and now had built back up his reserve to the point of
wanting to have some friends over to strut a little but couldn't
remember how to turn off his defences. As for example to keep the
edge in his voice from cutting something by accident, having to
sheath it in that darky act etcetera. He even kept the other vehicles
at a distance. When one wanted to stop at a brand of service station to match their credit cards they would begin honking and
headlight blinking and swing off whether we made the exit or not.
When we didn't we waited down the road; when we did make it
he still wouldn't join them at the pumps because he burned diesel
fuel. He didn't pull in for a fill-up until we'd wound up clear  on
over the Siskiyou Pass and into Weed. The others stopped at the
cafe and had coffee and watched us through the window. And no
credit cards for him; he paid cash out of a little suede bag hung
with a little notebook over the steering wheel shaft. He told me it
was their cut of the collections and donations from the Worship
Fair, and he wrote the amount down in the notebook with the ivory
hair-arrow the tip of which was a modern ballpoint pen. If he
wasn't back in the bosom of his bus tending to something he'd
just sit tight in the driver's seat fooling with the earphones or going over that notebook, making it very obvious to the rest of our
caravan watching from the Coffee Shop that he didn't find it necessary to quit his fully-stocked rolling stronghold with all the con-
veniences from stereo to private plumbing. I could've stood a cup

but what the heck, I figured; when in Rome you might as well sit tight.

Before we pulled out of one place Uncle Ronald come to see what was the plans for lunch. Lunch? asks Keller-Brown; "Didn't I see the ladies carry on an ice chest and a bag *bulging?*" Sometimes he exaggerated his act making every syllable perfect so he was not just a darky but a darky with a diploma. "Literally *bulging?*"

Uncle Ronald wasn't impressed. "Jelly sandwiches and goat's milk," he growls through the unparted hedge of his whiskers; "And that motherawful yogurt." "You mean that isn't a lunch?" Keller-Brown asks and Uncle Ronald says "I mean that ain't barely a breakfast. And I had breakfast. I mean I want a *fry chicken & taters lunch* and there's one coming up right outside Red Bluff if my memory serves . . . and free, man, *free!*" Mr. Keller-Brown says "Thanks, man," softly, the sheath off for a cold instant, "but I would rather eat the mother yogurt. I *know* the free chicken your memory serves." Uncle Ron winces from the cut. His eyes spark and start to narrow but instead the big grin breaks out of the brush. "Montgomery, my man, wouldn't you say you let your neck get so stiff you cuttin off your belly?" This struck all of us funny, particularly Uncle Ronald, fighting down laughing to ask me "Wouldn't you say, Mrs. Whittier? A *soul*-brother who'd rather eat goat yogurt than free fried chicken. . . wouldn't you say he must got something against his belly?" "Either that," I say, "or against free fried chicken. . . ?" Keller-Brown says he has nothing against chicken and I scratch my head and say "Well, then maybe he's got something against the fried chicken *frier*—" At this, Uncle Ron's laughter finally erupts from his holding it back. It come shooting up out of his back-thrown face and shoves him clear back down the steps. He goes staggering towards their bus, whooping up an absolute bouquet. I didn't know what I'd said that was so funny, but I couldn't help joining in. Even Mr. Keller-Brown unstiffened and chuckled a little as he maneuvered the big machine out of the truckstop and over the cement. "What Ron found so amusing, Mrs. Whittier, is this chicken frier is my wife's daddy." "Oh *ho*," I say. "And you'd rather eat yogurt . . . ?" "Than take a handout from my daddy-in-law. Rat on, Miz Whittier, o my *yes!*" Shifting down into the minstrel mock of his predicament smooth as putting his bus into a lower gear for the grade out of the mountains. "Ah druther eat fishworms, ah druther eat *blowflies. . .*"

But he did turn off the freeway outside Red Bluff towards a big new Charcoal Charlie's Chicken 'n' Fixin's, the fanciest one I ever saw, with a gift shop, a two-story-'round-a-pool Modern Motel and a miniature golf course, the last hole of which the golfer had to putt up a red-carpetted tongue through the open bucktoothy grin and down the dark gullet of a giant plastic Charcoal Charlie head. And in the restaurant itself there was a charcoal pit you could have barbecued a streetcar on. Far as the eye could penetrate there were chicken halves by the dozens smoking under the bucktoothed softeyed inspection of a lifesize plastic Charlie doll dressed in his trademark outfit of boiled white shirt and tattersall vest and tummy tied round and back around with the strings of his trademark floursack apron. The doll was standing at the end of the pit, hands clasped behind his back and bent a little forward in a attitude gentle but judicious, nodding approval at all that automatic chickenturning gadgetry flipping parched pullet halves past him. After every complete cycle of his nodding pivoting inspection, the head would stop and lean back, nose lifting and eyelids pulling down like oilcloth windowshades, make a long satisfied sniffing sound then broadcast the Charcoal Charlie slogan from hinged lips: "Raise um back home cook um downsouth and serve um uptown yah *suh!*" Ron says Tell it like it is, Papa Char, and led us on past the pit into the Easter weekend dining room mob. Actually, I felt less gaped at than I usually do crossing a crowded restaurant. Normally I'm a sight to really stick in the craw of a roomful of diners looking up to see me coming in amongst normal folks; now, amongst this crazyquilt group squeezing into a booth I felt myself more a part of an interesting spectacle than a disfigured eyesore.

There was eight in our party, not including Mr. Keller-Brown who had stayed on the bus to eat yogurt and deepbreathe and keep an eye on Otis—a full parade. Besides Toby and me, and Uncle Ronald practically booming out of his wool sweater and beard, there was Uncle Ron's wife (Mrs. Keller-Brown's younger sister) who was a sweet little thing named Chastity but, owing to her own prominent characteristics booming out of her own sweater, called by only half of it by her spouse; and Charmaine, the third girl singer, a thin girl with a generous mouth, shiny collarbones and a neck like an antelope; and Charmaine's boyfriend, a scraggly little mongrel who was the only other whitefolks along, called

Larry the Lugger because he was in charge of lugging their para-
phernalia on and off stages (when Ron introduced him to me as
the group's Token Boy, Larry said very testily, It takes more than
a boy to carry them amps and junk. Ask Charmaine if it don't. She
says *Miles* more, Larrylove. . . smiling open-mouthed down
from her stalk of a neck and winking to the rest of us as much as
to confide that she could swallow Larrylove with half a glass of
water); and cranky old Background their booking agent and manager; and Mr. Keller-Brown's wife, Levity. Chastity says there
was five kids in the Charles family and they nearly all had them
kind of names. She said the first and eldest brother was named
Priority but let run a little too wild while Mother and Father
Charles started their first charcoal pit in Tampa. "Priority is now
doing ten to life for Armed Assault in a Florida pen, whereas the
*second* son who was named Veracity did turn out to be a successful business lawyer in the same state. So that handle fit. Then
comes lovely Levity, then sweet little me . . . " I didn't say so
but the handle "Levity" didn't look to me like it was any better fit
than what had been hung on poor unfortunate Priority. She was
pretty, prettier than her younger sister, and had a pleasant enough
smile when she spoke to me or Toby or the waitress, but when the
smile left that trouble between her and Keller-Brown would
swarm right back into her face like a cloud of mean gnats. I ask,
"Say then, Mrs. Keller-Brown, if I may pry,"—to try and cheer
her up: "What did they call the fifth one? Finality?" She shakes
her head No, that she doesn't remember what it was called, and
looks down at her salad about as cheered up as if I'd used a wreck-
er's pry. Chastity comes to my rescue and says she thinks he was
called Baby Boy Charles on the records and never anything more;
"Because immediately after delivery he was rushed to surgery
with an unformed frontal skull and never survived." I say I'm
sorry. Chastity shrugs and says "The whole family got brainier
with each new kid, as you can plainly see by little number four.
Number five just had more grey matter than his little head could
hold." I say that must've been it. The little boy is following every
word and I'd like to change the subject. "Four out of five ain't
bad," Uncle Ronald says. "Three, actually," Chastity says: "If
we're honest about poor Priority. In fact, on closer examination of
the Charcoal Charlie flock, *none* of the roosters was that big a success . . . " "That's a shame," I say. I like her. I like the way
she bubbles up and tell her, "But they more than made up the dif-

ference with the hens." "Why, do you think so . . . ? she teases, preening, as his brow goes back and forth. It is extra big sure enough. "Do you think so, honestly?" "Honest injun," I say: "prize stock . . . " "I got to agree," she says, preening again and Uncle Ronald says "You hens better watch this crowing," and everybody laughs except the child. We bounce this around some. From me to her to him his face goes, back and forth, alert and comprehending, chock full of brains plainly enough but as empty of expression or opinion or interest even, curiosity even, as that doll's head watching the chickens broil . . .

Uncle Ron and Chastity kept the banter going. They made a real Burns and Allen, only merrier. He was from some Island in the South Seas and had a British accent that got higher and sped up faster the longer he tried to make his sentences, until he would stumble to a stuttering stop, then she would mock him about it and tell him to take it easy. He would come back about her Florida drawl: "Baby what you call easy I call *retired!* I'm a *young* cat ain't I now? and a young cat's better steppin' fast kickin' dirt and stumbling occasionally than having his tongue retired to a wheelchair on the Tampa Boardwalk isn't 'e now? "Yeah, Baby, but when you-all's kickin dirt you get it in your eye teeth and you can't see what you're *saying* . . . " And so forth until tears was coming down my cheeks. Mrs. Keller-Brown was tickled right up out of her doldrums; even old Background started putting in a cranky comment here and there. It was so contagious by the time our orders arrived the whole restaurant was swept up in this couple's merrymaking.

All I got was giblets with rice and coleslaw, 99 cents. The others had ordered the most expensive fare on the bill. Uncle Ron got both the New York Cut with full dinner plus the Barbecued Cornish ala carte. "Better belly up, Grandma," he says: "Might not be nothing else but goat yogurt till we get to Vegas. It don't cost us nothing here because we got a *pass*, dontcha see . . . We pass the tab onto Papa Charcoal and Papa passes it on to his tax lawyer who passes out." So I order a cup of egg custard for dessert (though what I was really dying for was a second cup of coffee, but I knew better from the trouble I was having sleeping) and a little platter of pink and vanilla ice cream wafers. Smokes were lit up. Larry the Lugger took Toby to the juke box. I picked at the custard with the wafers while Uncle Ron and Background leaned back and regaled our booth and most of the others with tales of their one-niter jazzband pasts. It was real entertaining. And the ladies chimed in here and there just like the chorus they were. Now and then everybody was talking at once. You could see why the Birds of Prayer was so popular for a gospel group. They did know how to have a ball! They could get it going and bounce and juggle and spin it from one to the other like one of them colored clown basketball teams. It was a kind of floor show; Papa Charlie must have made back the price of our meal just on the extra desserts bought to linger over around the room. Then, all at once, the other customers weren't looking at us anymore; something out the window behind our booth was more fascinating. The whole place was turned to watch, grins and goodfellowship all going fast. Mr. Keller-Brown had put on a big loose orange robe and was out in the fairway, positioned between the miniature windmill and the open gullet final golf hole. He had his feet spread and his arms out and looked like some kind of daylight spook swimming in slow motion in an invisible river. Or wrestling with the wind. It was very controlled and graceful, but all the more spooky for it. The diners were beginning to mutter, and our table to grit and fidget. "M'kehla's into his Tai Chi," says Chastity; "that means he must be finished with his mantra and his breath of fire." "And his goat curds," Uncle Ronald adds. "Then let's go," says Larry the Lugger, ears turning red with the thought of all these people beginning to associate us with that weirdy; "before he gets to his snake dance." And on the way past the cash register when the girl asks What's your friend got Background says "Nothin'. Plenty a *nothin'* . . . "

We lined out south again. Toby went to his desk and I dived into the waterbed. I was absolutely exhausted yet still simply could not doze off for all my turning down that second cup of coffee. I kept wondering, Why do they put up with him? He's no worldbeater of a musician nor winner of any popularity contests whereas they got everything: talent, personality, all daddy's credit cards . . . plenty of everything. I joggled along flat on my back puzzling this. Out the windows the sky was blue and the sun shone down and the tops of the telephone poles whanged past. I shut my eyes but the shadows of the phone poles beat right through: whang! whang! whang—like a sleeping remedy, kind of primitive but surely and steadily beating the brain senseless. *Whang whang whang whang!* The first time Emerson went to butcher a bacon hog on our new Nebo property he found—after getting the scalding tub a-boil and the knives all sharp on the plank table and the neighbors gathered to help hoist—that he didn't have no gun but the .22 and no shells but those little navy-bean-sized .22 shorts for target-practice. And that sow weighed better than 400 lbs. . . . *Whang whang whang whang!* It took the whole cartridge tube and half another. Then even so the miserable beast come to during the scalding! It went to squealing bloody murder and kicking around in the air till it kicked loose of the hoist and took off running around on the ground. Not away, not off to the trees, but just around the yard, snuffling around the fire and the tree while the crows called and the poles went past and the neighbors made Emery so nervous he like to never got the tube re-filled. The sow on the other hand had got peaceful to the point of getting her appetite back. By the time poor Emerson T. was loaded and cocked and situated again to open fire anew on her already-riddled skull the sow had found the clotted puddle left by the first volley and was calmly lapping it up out of the dusty yard.

I didn't get up again till nearly night. The bus was parked in a rest area and the sky out the windows was down to the last dregs of a flatland twilight. I smelt pastry baking and raised up to see Mr. Keller-Brown at the galley chopping vegetables by the light of one oil lamp turned low. If you kept that light that low for my benefit, I told him, you deserve to chop a finger off. He says it was no trouble; he'd put supper in to cook before the daylight faded and was just puttering around now while it cooked. Ooof, I grunt, trying to get up . . . "So you're a chef too. It sure smells delectable. I'll lend you a hand—soon as I can get out of this blessed quagmire. Oof and damnation! There ain't nothing to push against . . . " He had to come back and help me, pulling me up by one hand to keep me from tottering . . . "I'd like your expert's opinion on this, Mrs. Whittier . . . " He turned me loose and stooped to open the purple porcelain door of that range's cute little oven. Using his apron as a potholder he stood with the cake I had smelled; he brandished it for me to examine, proud as a frog eating fire. "It looks like a prizewinner—Mr. Keller-Brown . . . Angel food?" "Sponge," he said, "Eighteen egg sponge." I told him then I'd have to reserve judgment till it was sliced so I could squeeze a piece close to my ear. "Everybody knows one of

156

the ways you judge a sponge cake is by how it sounds. What we better do *first off* is loosen the edges. If it sticks it'll pull out pieces as it cools and that'd be a crying shame. If you'll show me where's a knife . . . " "Be my guest," he says and tips his head down for me to get that ivory outfit out of his hair. I start to say something about sanitation but when I pull the quills lo and behold out comes a long thin knife shiny as a dime, leaving the ivory scabbard still in his hair. "First a comb then an inkpen now a little sword cane. What else can it do?" He says its also good at getting itches in the middle of your back and olives out of the bottom of an olive jar. He holds the cake while I run the little blade around the sides and middle. "One and a half dozen eggs," I say; "what's the occasion for such a splurge?" He says that cake of mine yesterday reminded him that today was the day for Toby's celebration. Why, I says, I had the idea he was born in the fall, and he says, No they named him October because he had Scorpio rising, but his birth sign is Sagittarius. Sagittarius? I ask. With Scorpio *rising*! He yipes, flipping the cake upside-down onto a cutglass dish and sucking his hand where it finally burned him through the apron. I tell him Mr. Keller-Brown I hate to be a wet blanket on such a pretty birthday cake, but you're approximately three months late if he's born a Sagittarius. He went into his educated voice: "A lot of cultures, Mrs. Whittier, both eastern and western, celebrate—as well as the birth*day*—the *night* nine months earlier. Understand?" He gave me a look to see if I did. I told him I was ancient alright but still in possession of at least some notion how the birds and bees tended to business. And, with that, picked up my overnight case excused myself and started down the bus stairwell, nose in the air. Just fooling of course to shame him a little for talking down to a illiterate of any sort, even a geriatric, but my stupid feet were still asleep and I slipped and tripped and would have plopped clear out the door to the parking lot pavement and a fractured hip if he hadn't snagged me. His hand flicked out like the tongue of a big old bullfrog the flies thought dozing. He passed me to help me on down, swirling around in front of me then guiding me like a thistle, a hand cool on my waist and another light under my elbow. I thanked him in a fluster and told him if I could ever save his life just let me know. He looked at me, his eyes clouded with thinking. He says now that I mention it, he could use a little favor . . . Listening, I say, Anything the Good Lord and a bad old back will let me bear. He says it's a mission

157

needing diplomacy and wisdom, not a young back . . . "You won't have to bear anything heavier than a white flag, Mrs. Whittier." I tell him Nothing to it, that I'd been flag bearer for as many truces as Carter has pills. He wanted me to approach the group in his behest and tell them he'd like them, like *all* of us to honor his bus by coming in for supper and cake. "Especially my old lady, you understand? My wife . . . ?" Sincere and straightforward, and touching, too, the way no effort was made to hide the confession of guilt and despair and failure implicit in such a request. "You understand what I mean . . . ?" It was no place for monkeying around so I just nodded Yes, I understood . . . squeezing his hand back and promising him that I would do my dadgumdest. Then on off towards the flagstone house marked Fresno County LADIES I floated, my head humming like a hive and my tongue already working up the honey of my tidings that the neck has unstiffened and the heart softened and Mr. Keller-Brown begs reconciliation and has prepared a nice supper and celebration to seal the reunion. I rehearsed it a dozen ways in front of the mirror and prayed on the stool that I'd be successful; it *was* an important mission. I came out of the bathroom refreshed rehearsed and ready, and headed across to the group sitting under the mercury light around a parktable full of empty yogurt cups and apple cores gnawed narrow. It couldn't be too hard convincing them that hot meat and vegetables and sponge cake was a better deal than goat yogurt. Even sobersided Mrs. Keller-Brown . . . I'll charm the socks off her! Anyways I was so infatuated with my assignment that it wasn't until I seen the child's face beaming blue-eyed at me from where he was harbored under her arm that it dawned on me what night he'd sent me to ask her to come celebrate.

They all was happy to come, though, and I figured let him explain the occasion for the cake. While Uncle Ron toted the ice chest to their bus Chastity lends me her arm back across the lot. She also tells me how glad she is I come along and what a splendid influence I been on the situation. I told her well I don't know about that but I always did kind of fancy myself a diplomat. She says I was just what was needed to ease tensions in this cold war —a regular Henry Kissinger: "I know that damn invitation indicates a real warming trend," she chirrups. I says I hope she's right and ask how long had it been froze up. She says since Christmas, nearly half a year. Now I *know* it hadn't taken Keller-Brown no four years to notice that he and his black-eyed bride had whelped a suspiciously blue-eyed pup so I make so bold as to ask her what she thought had set it off . . . somebody find out something new on the other? She grins impish at me and says No, not to her knowledge. "Sister Lev swear she's Bo'n Again no mo' to sin," she says, and I say I'm glad. She says nobody knows what happened because nothing was ever said; "But I *personally* couldn't help but notice that it coincided with a barrage of tests they give Toby at the Standford University. Everybody knew he was far out but not just how far. The testers, three little Jewish dudes, come all the way to Oakland with the boy and the results; they wanted to hire him for study. M'kehla sent them hurrying. First the old one, then the two that thought they might have a better chance persuading us because they were *longhaired* even if they was shrinks. Then, the next morning, Lev packs into our bus. And the cold war's been on ever since." I shake my head. Finding out your offspring has a big I.Q. don't sound like grounds to start a cold war, I says. She says maybe not; but it sure might stimulate some new ideas about custody.

He'd elaborately frosted the cake by the time we filed into his lamplit spread. And when he did explain, at the end of just a fantastic feast, he announced it simply as "Toby's *Chun*-day" in an Oriental twang I couldn't tell whether anybody translated or not. Everybody'd been pretty puzzled-looking about the whole business and their faces didn't change much when he explained that a Chun-day cake didn't have candles because it wasn't an anniversary of the coming out into the light like a birthday cake. But he had Toby make a silent wish anyway then let him slice it with that miniature sword. Keller-Brown dished up the wedges and served them to us with tiny cups of coffee. (I got the first piece naturally and after sniffing and tasting and rolling a piece gently between thumb and forefinger next to my ear for the tiny bubbles bursting moist yet firm, told him it was a blueribbon at any fair. Everybody agreed. Even Otis, who'd come to enough to mournfully join us. Toby said he'd eat his later because he was full from cutting it, the pieces always sticking to his fingers. While Toby licked his hands Uncle Ron took down a ukelele and begin to pick melodies on it and his wife leaned against him and warbled and tweeted along like a robin redbreast. The lamps fluttered and everything was nice and cordial. "Hey wouldn't this be a right time to have Toby do us a page?" Mr. Keller-Brown asks; "It's been a while . . . " Everybody nods except Larry the Lugger who wants to know "Outta your book I suppose?" Keller-Brown looks at him but Larry is bent over his paper plate very involved with dessert. Mr. Keller-Brown says you got a beef with my Bible, Lawrence? Larry looks out the window then; finally he says, "The pages in yours are too long, man. We got to get to L.A. in time to set up." So Mr. Keller-Brown says they'll use a smaller edition; who's got a smaller edition handy? Ron? Lev? Anybody? Then he looks at me. Of course I had my redletter edition in my overnight case and he knew it. He'd seen me reading it. I got it and Mr. Keller-Brown unzipped it and knelt in the light beside the low table. "You better wash your hands, before touching a book like this, Tobe." While the little fella was obeying, Keller-Brown browsed through it pointing along at certain illustrations with the scabbard. The boy washed and the folks waited, silent and attentive, and expectant like they was familiar with this ritual. K-B explained to me that the Birds of Prayer use the Bible as a kind of group oracle. "A book like this," he says as he points into the pages, "is bound to afford us a more inspiring oracle than for instance a deck of cheap Tarot cards . . . wouldn't you say?" I told him I didn't know much about such things, fortune cookies being about my limit, but I was sure whatever Toby read was bound to be inspiring. He laughed and snapped the pages shut. He held out the book and the little boy took it and sat on the floor, squinching his eyes closed tight. Keller-Brown says soft and ceremonious, "While Toby reads who's into a foot massage? Mrs. Whittier? The source of most bad backs is the metatarsus, you know. Go ahead Tobe; when you're ready . . . "

The child held the book in his lap, eyes shut, tiny hands moving over the old blackleather cover embossed Mr. and Mrs. E. T. Whittier, then with a swoop opened it and looked down to see what he'd turned to: "Hosea," he reads aloud from the top of the pages as his daddy slips off my shoes. "Hosea, Chapter Two . . . " I think to myself *Hosea? Hosea?* And he intones, " 'Say ye Say ye unto your brethren Am-me and to your sisters Ruehama . . . ' "
—reading and enunciating painstakingly while I'm thinking Hosea- surely Lord you can provide better balm for this tender rend finally on the verge of healing back together than Hosea! Somebody oughta say something, make a motion to turn to a better passage than this. Hosea Chapter Two will splatter this warm occasion to pieces like a shower of icewater . . . But nobody

made any such motions; nothing moved except the father's hands going from one foot-rub to the next and the little boy's voice working deliberately down the page, tolling each word reverently like some cherub ringing down a judgment he respected even if he didn't understand . . .

" 'Plead with your mother, plead for she is not my wife, neither am I her husband: let her therefore put away her whoredoms out of her sight and her adulteries from between her breasts; lest I strip her naked and set her as in the day that she was born and make her as a wilderness, and set her like a dry land, and slay her with thirst. And I will not have mercy upon her children; for they be the children of whoredoms. For their mother hath played the harlot; she that conceived them hath done shamefully: for she said, "I will go after my lovers, that give me my bread and my water, my wool and my flax, mine oil and my drink." Therefore behold I will hedge up thy way with thorns and make a wall, that she shall not find her paths.' " Tolling on and on those terrible curses right down to " 'And now will I discover her lewdness in the sight of her lovers, and none shall deliver her out of mine hand. I will also cause her mirth to cease, her feast days, her new moons —' " There he stopped. It was the bottom of the page. He shut the book and looked back up at his dad.

"That was fine, Tobe." Mr. Keller-Brown's voice was husky and his cheeks were wet with weeping. "Wasn't it, folks?" Everybody muttered yeah great, real good Toby . . . except Mrs. Keller-Brown. She set like a zombie, staring at her bare feet still shining with oil from her husband's hands and her yellow bellbottoms dotted with his tears. She was swallowing and sniffing too. I felt a lump hop into my throat and my vision got watery looking on them. The whole bus was choked up with the shared sense of something accomplished, something resolved after a long painful time.

I seen then what it was made them follow after him. Maybe he wasn't so gifted on the drums or much fun to neighbor with but, as he knelt there at his wife's feet, the Bible in his hand and the look of lonely righteousness crackling around his eyes as he went from face to face—asking no pity! daring denial!—I seen that it would take more than just an ordinary power *not* to follow him . . .

They wouldn't let me help with dishes so I crawled back into the waterbed with Toby and a loop of string to show him the Jacob's Ladder and Crowsfoot. Otis followed us with Keller-Brown's orange robe clutched around as much of his chicken-wired pink flab as it could cover. He stood ogling us and I thought for a horrible moment he was going to join us in the waterbed but instead he slunk up into the recline-o-lounger and watched us from there like a starved stray through a kitchen screen on Christmas morning. Once he whispered in a kind of broken croak: "Doughnuts go gentle into that good night, Varooshka!" and another time: "Tell me, why poor little Otis?" That was all. But he watched us all the time, pleading with that starved stray expression that he wanted to ask for lots more if we'd just open the screen and let him in. I was glad for the pitiful thing that he was at last coming out of his tailspin enough to make some contact, but his gooney gawking bothered me nonetheless. So as soon as the bus got rolling and the little boy got busy with the string and stretched out to get cozy I did the same though I *still* was not what you could call drowsy by a long shot. Play sleeping to keep from meeting looks with him. Like you'll playlike having to cross the street to see an acquaintance but really to keep from meeting looks with a legless pencil vendor on the sidewalk ahead, not that you begrudge a dime or couldn't use a new pencil but that you can't help but fear a dime *can't* be all he's after—shortchanged as bad as he clearly is! —and those pencils are whittled sharp as daggers if he don't get at least *better*. I could feel his eyes whimpering at me till I wanted to stick my head under the covers but I kept still, pretending to sleep. So maybe Mr. Keller-Brown *is* a little pushy on the sly. Didn't Emerson T. send off for them Rosicrucian lessons and wasn't I tempted to read them? And what if he's got a peacock's temper when something disturbs his strut? At least he ain't gonna whimper. He aint gonna whine and beg and bite when the handout *runs* out, I says in my mind, like *some* curs I could name. And kept my eyes closed to that whimpering nor turned over to help the little fingers trying to find which string went where. Sure he's concerned for custody. His kid's a treasure. Did any of *my* young read at the age of four and a half, mind like an angel and have the actual Eye of Prophesy guiding their hand? So Dad struts his stuff or covers himself like a darky he's a man for it all and probably a lot stronger father than Emerson T. was, God forgive me for saying so. And I couldn't help but be more charmed and impressed by him as things went along. By himself he had girded his loins and guided his tribe through a dark journey very impressively, pulling us into Los Angeles with hours to spare. Uncle Ronald and Chastity and Background and Larry traded off but he drove that rig the whole thousand miles without asking for or looking like he needed somebody to spell him. I had to marvel at him, and when I finally made it up out of that waterbed somewhere about San Fernando I walked right up to tell him so.

Otis was up and around for the Los Angeles approach. Still in the orange robe he was sitting with his feet in the stairwell lip-reading a newspaper by the light of a candle he was holding. Wax was all over his whole hand like a cocoon. Mr. Keller-Brown opened the campstool up for me. "How was the ride, all in all?" he asked. All I could see in the rearview mirror was his grinning teeth and eyes. "All in all it was just fine," I says; "Just like dreaming you're going somewhere and waking up actually there." "I'm gratified," Keller-Brown says. "Me too," I say. "Lebanon bleeds!" croaks Otis, reading aloud to nobody in particular, just trying to get his two cents rallied and back in . . . "Israel forces *attack* six villages in retaliatory raids chanting '*Revenge! Revenge!*' for the eighteen jews killed by Lebanese Terrorists. Call *that* dreaming!" Mr. Keller-Brown nor me neither acts like we've heard. Otis drops to a mumble down the bus stairwell and Mr. Keller-Brown asks me if I'd like to make a stop. I say I'm alright awhile yet. He says we've just got to swing by Otis' house to drop him off then straight on to the hotel reserved for us in Hollywood. Another twenty minutes. I say, "I can stand it if you can." Otis riles up, reading "Female soldiers carry wreaths lead the procession for the eighteen victims, wailing and tearing at their flesh till the blood ran." "Think of that," says Keller-Brown. "Till the blood *ran!*" he squawks, back to us: "Is that any way for a soldier to act?" "Not in my opinion," I humor him, then whisper to Keller-Brown "Are you sure he ought to be turned loose like this?" He answers that he's sure at Otis' home there will be hot bath full fridge and such comforts waiting, along with his family or friends who will probably be familiar with this. "Lebanese villagers ask why?!" Otis croaks, rending the paper in a furious attempt to turn the pages with his one un-waxed hand. "Why you? Why me? Why *any*body!" The paper billows everyplace. "A hot bath a cold beer and a fresh newspaper," Keller-Brown reassures me.

But when we stopped to let him out there was nothing but the newspapers, and none of these fresh—piled and un-opened and the subscription cancelled weeks ago for lack of payment. The porchlight was on but it hadn't stopped the neighborhood hooligans from busting in and tearing up holy ned inside and leaving spraypainted on the picture window "THE CRISCO YID GETS YOUR MEAT GOLDEN BROWN." The men all milled around the front stoop talking it over while Otis picked through the yellow newspapers with his bare big toe. Every few seconds one of them would stick his head inside and flick on the light and look around, then shut the light off and they'd talk about it some more. Finally Chastity reached somebody on a neighbor's phone, a brother who promised to drive right over, and we left. As we drove away I watched out the rear window; far as I could see he stood there right like we'd left him, in the sorry clutter of his house, just inside his busted door in nothing but his filthy shorts now that Keller-Brown had took back his robe, his back and shoulders and legs patterned like the inlaid floor of a bus station lavatory.

Sad a sight as it was, all of us couldn't help but heave a relieved sigh getting loose from that mess before it got any stickier. Keller-Brown said he hoped he'd be alright, that we would've waited if things weren't so tight—"We're only going to get about two hours rest as it is!" I told him not to worry; that the Good Lord looks after kids fools and drunks and Otis qualifies on all three counts.

We got to the hotel and there was people right out front waiting for us, still or already; they took our luggage and parked his bus and such while a girl in a tweed suit took about a thousand flash pictures. The van with Background and the second bus with Larry driving both headed right on out to the Bowl to prepare things and the rest of us hurried on up to our rooms to get what rest we could before the show. Toby cried getting woke up in his daddy's arms and said he wanted back on the bus. Keller-Brown told him the bus was parked under the hotel and he could have a little room all his own. He said he didn't want any such thing; he wanted to sleep with his daddy. "Not tonight," Keller-Brown says; "No room." "Why?" the little feller wails sleepily; "Why didn't you rent a bigger bed?" "It's the biggest bed in the house," Keller-Brown says. I got it then. "You can sleep with Granma, Honey Lamb," I says. He thought it over and decided it would do. Keller-Brown carried him into my room behind the bellboy and laid him on the bed. "Thanks," he says to me; "For understanding . . . Thanks and good night." He took my hand and squeezed. I squeezed back and says "You're very welcome and . . ." because I saw his wife coming up the hall, head-heavy with lack of sleep and who knows what overload of soul-searching after that scolding from Hosea "good luck." He smiled and pulled my door shut behind him.

The little boy was asleep by the time I come back out of the bathroom. I scooted him over and made myself a place but I didn't lay down. Exhausted as I was my mind was jumping around like a grasshopper eating ripe tobacco. And my heart thumping from a sincere handholding! And the little boy breathing deep and easy and in no mysterious danger after all! And the Hollywood Bowl at Sunrise and after that who knows! "Rebecca," I says; "you better calm yourself if you don't want the hives." That made me remember the bee sting. And that prompted me to read a little before I laid down. I pulled me a chair over to the only window my room had, a set of big french doors opening onto the least little balcony I ever saw. Just big enough to fit one lawnchair on and not another blessed thing. And when I tried to push them open with my foot I saw that the lawnchair kept them from parting more than to let through perhaps the skinniest of starlets. The *silliest* arrangement! And down on the sidewalk across the way a statue would light up so every so often when a car passed . . . of some crazy creature turning round and around all to the empty street. I just had to shake my head and laugh: "What a world" and kept looking up from my book every time a car went past to ponder and chuckle over whatever it was toe-dancing down there or recall to savor the way he smiled at me, so I never even noticed what page I had unknowingly and innocently opened to till I licked my thumb to turn it and well, *there's* one thing else, Mr. Keller-Brown, that your little utility hairpin can be used for . . . a ivory saltshaker. What other undisclosed talents does *this* little genius boast behind that angel's brow snoozing away? Angel my foot! Disguised demon more like. I know I ought to take steps in behalf of the child's shady soul *but I puzzled what's to be done? His hide's done been tanned. Even say I try to take step who'd believe such a boogeyman whopped of justification about such a charmer of a daddy and his gifted little sugarplum of a shill? On the basis of one dead kittycat and a pinch of salt in Hosea who on earth would go along with whatever desperate measures I am soon going to either have to seriously consider or consummately put from my mind as just more of this city's silliness that seeped into my thinking without my*

They approached again, and for the third time stopped to stand on the other side of the bolted door. This time she rose from the chair. She put the Bible on the night stand and took her teeth from the glass. She clamped them into place and then turned to cross the rug and stand on her side of the door, plucking at the neck of her gown, giving her teeth a final adjustment. She thought of how it was like a refrigerator: the light will come on and show what's for breakfast—always sustenance but never what a fella really hungered after. Finally she breathed a resigned sigh and slid the bolt. She twisted the crystal knob and swung open the door, stepping back out of his way so he could shuffle in with his arm-load of fresh morning papers. He stopped after his entrance and swayed uncertainly in the apron of light like a drunken burlesque clown at the end of the runway, swaying and squinting to see if there's any audience before going into his routine. Unseen and silent, she shook her head at the sight. He was wearing green satin slacks and suitcoat of bright green satin with white shamrocks embroidered in the cuffs and lapels. Once the pride of any grand St. Patrick's celebration, the outfit was now so rumpled and soiled and illfitting that she finally had to tease aloud . . .

"Everything else wornout or outgrown, I suppose?"

He spun, startled by the voice so close behind him. Then he looked forlornly down at his attire. "I was Og the Leprechaun in *Finian's Rainbow.* It was the only thing they didn't steal, the scum . . ."

"Your neighbors?"

"No," he said, his mouth pouting and his voice shakily sarcastic. "My famous friends and family who were going to give me all that comfort and understanding and help me out of this hellpit that witchdoctor schvartze shoved me into. For no reason!"

"Hush, fool."

"No reason at —"

"Hush," she said and pushed him on into the room so she could shut the door. She passed him in the dark to the night stand across the room. When she switched on the lamp he was again startled and spun again in fright. She stood with her hands on her hips, shaking her head . . .

"Some answer to a lady's prayer!"

(to be continued)

166

Faye, Jed, Zane, Shannon — 1964

# Zane and Jed

I work at sitting still, at trying to see . . . I labor with my senses and the material at hand, to make sense . . . sand flies light on my feet and I flick my toes in recognition . . . yesterday I found a rock in a sunny and secluded little cove of sand, a stone created by Braque with quartz-white bird shapes soaring across a clay-blue sky, and I thought "I'll take this home and make a dias covered with black felt so the rock will be framed and spotlighted. In fact, I could collect a number of such stones and arrange them in an exhibit." Then, in a sudden anger of self-disgust, I gripped the stone instead, against the sun, against the sky, against the green backdrop of he sea—once, even, against my bare belly—and then chucked it as far into the surf as my arm could.

I collected no exhibits that day, but, for a moment there, I held a stone.

Now . . . I wrangle with the sun. That empty dias nags at my lazy ways. Up the beach I see Zane, white in his whiter shorts, make a defiant charge at the retreating edge of foam . . . and wonder:

What *is* it about a black felt background that demands us feed it light?

What is it that demands us labor with our joy?

And, again, I am tempted to create a paper stone, a plastic boy, and leave the things I love alone.

"Whatcha eatin', I ask Zane.
He wipes his mouth with a greasy wrist: "Bone," he says.

Jed, just humping up to all fours in preparation for his first
solo crawl, pauses a moment to grin at Anicin ad on TV . . .
Explaining to him PAIN . . . PAIN . . . PAIN

Responding, I open the workhouse door to see Zane, red sweat-shirt hanging inches below red jacket, come crying down the path from the woods.

"I was *Crying* for you," he says; as usual, stating the case with complete accuracy.

"I know," I tell him, "I heard you and came out to see."

"I was in the *woods*!" Tears pinker than his dirty face. "And I got *snot*."

"Were you scared?"

"Yeah," he nods, sniffing.

"Come here," I say.

And he comes.

"Why Plant Corn?" appeared among the boxes of material from which this book was drawn as notes from the author to himself. It represents many other partial and complete "notes" of this kind on various subjects. Each of these pieces, and especially, "Why Plant Corn?" seems to work out some thought process, some aspect of the way the world can be seen.

## Why Plant Corn?

Check the drive. Why plant corn? "Because I like to eat corn-stalks?" No. "Because I like corncobs?" No. "Because I like ("not even roasting ears with butter dripping off?" No, fool, you planted popcorn!) Then why? "to be COMFORTABLE!"

*Comfort* being the ball, meaning that from the enterprise I expect *no more* than a PIECE OF COMFORT. Ending up with an ear of strangelooking kernals that don't roast worth a damn and don't say "this is a failure because it isn't a roasting ear and it tastes *bad*, I try instead to say, "This ear of corn not behaving like any *I* ever seen before. Let's see if I like it to eat when it stops banging around."

Then, after the corn goes into the mouth

*How* does one know if he likes it or not?

Can't. Can only say "I like it maybe not so good as roasting ears with butter but like it heap more than grasshoppers."

Then, weighing as much information available, decide, all things considered, and in as I planted 80 acres, *I'll eat it.*

Then go at it, learning every way possible.

Where does this bring us?

I remember that *Not Doing* is all one accomplishes and is

practically the same as *Doing* only in reverse. *Not Doing*, i.e. *not thinking* about a burned hand, *not worrying* about getting a hard-on, *not looking* at the slaughter going on in every heart, *not thinking* about a Rhino . . . all the same, all putting us on the other side of the river from ourselves. Many times trying *not to listen* to a sound, or *not to look* at a sight, is the only way to perceive. As in watching a dim star, sometimes staring right at a thing obscures it until it's gone and can only be seen by looking way. There's a painting on the wall, an abstract piddle blue and white dip painting that I am *not* looking at, and the more I *don't* look at it the more my interest runs that direction, until by stopping writing and not looking at it concertedly for one minute ⸺

⸺⸺⸺⸺⸺⸺⸺⸺⸺⸺

⸺⸺⸺⸺⸺⸺⸺⸺⸺

⸺⸺⸺⸺⸺⸺⸺⸺

did so. Eyes closed, counted to 100, *found myself* accomplishing feats of *not thinking* about picture a time or two then swing back until it glowed very white at the edge of my dark room and finally *bam* opened my *eyes* AND! *dissappointment.*

I was expecting my *not looking* to bring about some optic miracle so when I looked I was by then not only *truly* not seeing the picture I was not even not seeing the optic miracle!

Expectations; "This green stuff *should* taste like sherbet" . . . (little realizing it tastes exactly like fried chicken)" Whoa; that's *bad*."

The expectation presupposes a "correct" way for the event to turn out. Anything other than the "correct" or "lime sherbet" taste is "Wrong." Anything wrong is "bad."

"Bad!" The tongue has been cheated. The eye, the stomach. The being walks away spitting in disgust, one green fried chicken the poorer.

*A fuller harvest with less expectation.*


More of the centipedes learning once more to dance, it brings us there at least.

Where else?

Back to *not looking* at the painting.

No; more yet. Back to *proving nothing,* to *wait don't wriggle* *etc.*

All these rules which lead (I think I remember) to *there is no rule.*

All these bench marks that rattle and ring in my memory but do not, *cannot* link up to the goal, the *the Cool Place* . . . because, somehow, paradoxically they are themselves that take the eye from the *ball*!

Yet they must be learned. And forgotten. Or the centipede will die a cripple.

To dance, fall down first.

The wiseman is the *fool* when he is *the* fool and through the *fool* finds his cool again.

The follow through after the change.

The Catcher hits, direction changes, he hits again direction changes, again direction changes, but by doing this . . . oh, just watch

"Bad!" The tongue has been cheated. The eye, the stomach. The being walks away spitting in disgust, one green fried chicken the poorer.

A fuller harvest with less expectation.

Then again splendid the pa...

Hope How to is

Does one cut down on what is perhaps the very that planted the corn?

*Chapter called* "Don't wrestle with a tarbaby..." *just now picked out of old North Beach novel called "ZOO" that I claimed was never puplished because, at that time, five or so years ago: The name*

*'beatnik' has too much meaning now in the public eye — too much to overcome. I think..." I have been heard to say "...I'll wait a number of years for the heat bit to die down before I bring it out." Bullshit. I didn't publish it 5 years ago because nobody bought it. I didn't publish it after success brought requests for it because I kept telling myself I would someday re-write it, bring it up to my present standards (like who wants their old adolescent bumbles marring the grace of present mature standards and fucking up a hard-won reputation?).*

We passed brown, two-room shacks with pigs under the porch, chickens in the broken windows and TV antennas on the roof. We passed bitter, parched fields where hawks hovered over the stubble waiting for little animals to make mistakes. ~~There was some variety in the scene; one~~ *little variety; one* house would be covered with tarpaper while its neighbor would be covered with chickenwire and sheetrock ~~—but there was~~ even a tameness in the ~~cooked almost lifeless~~ *In the miles since turning off 99* variety. ~~I saw through the~~ *lone man walking in the ditch along- some dirty symbol,* side the road, pulling a long pole behind him to some relentless plan. His big red wrists and neck bulged against his burden, and we left our dust to settle on his shoulders as we slammed past.

"Look at him *back* there," I said, *turning again to watch Wilson at the wheel.* "You'd think he was nailed to that pole the way he's working at it."

"They come on pretty serious down here," Wilson *said* ~~laughed~~. ~~"I've~~ *"My lummox of a brother..?I've watched him* ~~watched my big dumb brother~~ get so hung with some little incidental — ...*checker* with a game or blasting out a stump, something completely without *of how ridiculous he is.* importance - that he loses all sight. You'll see when we get there. *It's a scene to stand back and see how ridiculous these people can* ~~it's a good idea just to watch these people and not get up too close~~ get."

It was difficult to fabricate a family for Wilson. During the time I had been rooming with him in The City he had spoken of his parents only *and only then because* once, when I tried to tell him about my ~~father and his hardset plans~~ *folks.* for me *the baby* 'Don't put those stories on me,' he said, "because there's nothing *new about none of them!* ~~unique about them - my~~ Jews; Old Folks. My Old Lady put a shackle on me one thousand miles long; it took me seventeen years to bust loose."

I knew his mother to be dead and I had *been content to* imagined the rest of the family with her, done with, pruned from his existence. ~~He~~ *Wilson* would avoid the burden of relatives the way he avoided Vicki or Carla or *the once that* plump matron hooking at him on the street with her Buddy Poppy Goodness: "Aren't you concerned, young man, for our disabled fighters of the *(like who wants their old adolescent bumbles marring the grace of present mature standards and fucking up a hard-won reputation?)*

176

This is a fragment of a novel, **Zoo,** written in the early sixties before **Cuckoo's Nest** and never published. On the left is a reproduction of the beginning of the chapter from which this was taken.

Hoover came from the coops, cradling a big rooster against his overalls. This rooster was white. I had noticed him before in one of the cages but had dismissed him as an old barnyard rooster; I noticed now he was hard and lean as the hounds. Hoover carried his chicken and did shuffling dances among the kids & dogs who jumped jealously for the chicken.

"Whatcha think of the Big White, Arnold?"

"He looks just like a thousand other roosters I've seen on my ranch. Not a damn bit different."

Hoover held the rooster out and look him over thoughtfully. "Well, he probably isn't much different, I reckon—he just got a chance." He stomped and cursed the hounds and fogged the dust about him. "I won't crate him, if it's all right with you, Arnold. Don't want him all tight and nervous."

"Put him in the back seat," I said.

Just before we left, all the boys came running to the car. They had found the snake, the very one that must have been killing the chicks. Wouldn't we take them to the fights with us as a reward? Can't do 'er, boys, Hoover told them; Dora has to run you all home in the station wagon now.

The red-headed boy held the snake just behind the neck and it was patient with its dusty obsidian stare. When the boy tossed it to the hounds it lay as it was dead while the hounds snuffed and pawed it; when the hounds lost interest and moved away it swivelled beneath the barn to safety.

"Are you just going to stand out there, man, or you going to get in and drive? Let's get things on the road . . ."

Hoover jabbered and laughed as we drove, pointing out the secret turn markers showing how to get to the fight. I drove slowly, coming almost to a full stop at the turns. The rooster blustered about the back seat, crowing arrogantly and dotting the upholstery.

"A picnic," Hoover explained, "has slasher fights and gaff fights. An' you can enter your bird in whichever one you fancy. Slasher fights use razor sharp knives on the left heel and *phhht!* one good kick and that's all she wrote. I don't have much use for the slashers on account I breed big sturdy birds with a good jump; my boys ain't so fast maybe but any damn one of 'em would charge hell with a bucket of water and keep runnin' back to fill the bucket. Here, Arnold, I'll put my jacket down for him back here. He's nervous and a might droppy." When he turned back around he freed a long Coca Cola belch and sighed. "I been savin' the Big White till I almost hate to fight him. He's only fought three times, an' that was in secret. Not a scratch on him. I been savin' him to clean up on those little bandy-legged Filipinos. He's got more scrap than ten o' their chickens. I'll run him against one of their favorites in a gaff fight an' bet him to the hilt. I'll pull in a hundred dollars for certain, maybe two. Hot *dog!*"

Wilson laughed and shook his head at his brother's exuberence. "A real tycoon, aren't you, Hoover?" Hoover was too lost in his anticipation to answer.

I expected the fights to be quietly hidden from the SPCA in some dark, cryptic barn, not right off the road in the center of a field with hundreds of parked cars and barbecue pits blazing and women and children relaxing in the shade of scrubby crabapples and even a little withered attendant directing the steady flow of old and dusty cars to their proper slots with a "Right here, sirs, right this way," and a corncob pointer. The fighting pits were the center of activity, covered by a ceiling of stretched burlap and fenced in by benches and haybales and brown, cheering men who stood with chicken down clinging to their whiskers and collecting in their nostrils. The field about the pits had been tramped absolutely smooth by the fan-belt soled shoes of the white farmers and the bare brown feet of the Mexicans and Filipinos; a fine dust, light and sifted as dirty flour, covered the packed ground. The crowd milled about the pits or the barbecue fires in painfully bright oranges and reds and yellows.

Hoover carried his rooster through the crowd and waved and

grinned at those who shouted welcomes to him. "Just brought him along for the barbecue," he said in answer to the gibes about his white rooster. The rooster nodded his respect to the pile of dead chickens the women were plucking. Wilson and I followed in Hoover's wake. We stopped at the low rail to watch a fight in progress.

"Them're slasher chickens," Hoover said. "See the knives. The black there is bad cut. You won't see much more outen him."

The smaller, red chicken calculated the black's stagger, bobbed his hackled neck, rose in a staff arc, and struck sideways with the four-inch sickle of steel tied to his left leg. "Aaaa," the crowd breathed, relaxing, satisfied. The black chicken stepped back, seemingly untouched, slanted his angry head at his tormentor for a charge, and fell in two pieces before he could get in a blow. The red chicken pecked the half with the head on it until the head stopped pecking back, then walked away. The bets were paid, the owners moved out after their birds, and another pair was being carried, armed, into the circle. As the fat, heavy-nosed Mexican carried his victorious red chicken from the ring I noticed that no stain of blood marred the terrible gleam of the knife strapped to the leg—it had been that fast.

My forehead was seared with movement and color; images coming through my eyes were branded onto my brain with a red hot needle. I had let myself watch too closely. I breathed shallowly to ease the pain and squinted until I saw only forms.

"That black was a good shuffler," Hoover said. "I've seen him win a lot of gaff fights. He never shoulda matched with that damn knife. Now . . . you boys wanta watch the next scrap or come with me to weigh in?"

"We'll go with you," I said.

By the scales I dimly saw an old grey-robed crone plucking the halves of the Black for the hot charcoal outside. Hoover edged her aside and set his White on the scale. It teetered arrogantly back and forth while the officials, two more middle-aged, rock-eyed Filipino Weird Sisters glared at the jiggling needle. "Six-one," the smaller of the two said, "Big White o' Hoover." and wrote it into her ledger. She pushed her brambled face close to the rooster to examine it for scars; while she peered beneath the feathers Hoover brushed its bobbing head lightly to reassure it.

"You won't find a mark on him. He never fought a match," he told them. "I sparred him maybe twicet. He's just a barnyard pullet, ladies, green as a gourd, as you see. I just thought I'd put him in the pit today so's to have something to barbecue later on."

The chicken's feathers gleamed like snow in the hot sun. It held its sleek, combless head in high defiance of the officials as they tried to interpret its worth. They looked at the chicken, then at Hoover hunkered in the dust, flipping rocks, whistling his schoolboy innocence. The women gauged the whistle and looked at each other and nodded. One of them pointed to a slatted crate atop the haybales.

"You fight that chicken."

Hoover looked. A big red head was thrust between the slats, jerking back and forth. He dropped his handful of pebbles, his jaw fell open in a gesture of titanic disbelief. "*That* chicken!" he wailed. "That *fiend!* Now ladies, surely you're joshin' me. We all've watched that devil kill ever'thing but a *bull* dog! What's wrong with you? He's . . . that big buzzard . . . got twenty, possibly *thirty* fights on him and I'll bet you my bottom dollar on it. Look . . . look at my little skinny white barnyard pullet here, pantin' in the sun, fresh from his first moult—don't you even want the little fella to get a lick in?"

"That chicken," the woman repeated grimly. "You take o' leave, Hoover. You don' fool nobody."

Hoover stood up and flapped the dust from his overalls. "Aaah, what the hell. Win a few lose the rest. I just want him for the barbecue anyhow. When's the gaffs start?"

We had twenty minutes before the slasher fights were over. I couldn't take watching another fight so we all went outside among the women and children around the barbecue fires. Hoover put the chicken back in my car and immediately started putting the rush on two creamy-skinned Mexican girls of maybe fifteen and sixteen. Wilson wasn't even amused any longer and wandered off to stand in the shade of the crabapples, determined not to take part. I felt I should follow him but I couldn't help thinking that I should go back and open the window of my car a little. It would get awfully hot in there with all the windows up.

The chicken was hopping nervously about, scattering the dust that had settled in the car with his wings. I opened the door a crack and reached inside to the window. He stopped jumping about and watched me intently; his eyes were wet and bright, like tiny black sparks. He stood motionless, watching me roll down the window a few inches. I wondered if some ageless instinct of his breed told him he was about to fight, about to be pitted against another bird where only one of the two would leave.

His head reared back as I touched his bright pink wattles, but he didn't spring away. The soft flesh was hot against my fingertips. The metal of the car door was hot where I leaned against it to reach inside. The air of the car was like wool. Who'd have thought . . . it could be so *damned* hot this late in the year? My head had started banging again. I wished we had brought some wine.

Hoover hoohawed me over to meet his two new sweethearts and I closed the door, leaving the chicken standing as if hypnotized where I had touched him. I walked to the barbecue and Hoover introduced me to the girls. They stood shyly on the tips of their tiny brown feet like two fleet little deer, ready to break and run at a movement. Hoover was trying to tame them with offers of food.

"Well . . . eef you say . . . I'll haf the chile relleno, hokay?"

"Sure, hey guyss, thass fine, me too."

Hoover waved his happy wallet. "Bring us *all* some, *mamacita*, of whatever the stuff is they're askin' about. Some for Arnold, too. Wilson, come on over here an' you meet these two fine friends o' mine. This one is Nita and this one is Rita or Lita or somethin' like that. Look at those little brown melons there, boys; ready and ripe, what'd'ya say?"

The girl raised a shy hand to the top of her dress. "Oh, *you!* Oh you *guyss!*"

Hoover leered and stroked the plump butter of Something Like That's forearm. She drew away from him and took my arm and tried to engage me in a discussion of the fight.

". . . an' such a lot of *worry* over a cheeken, hey? Over a Sunday afternoon deener?"

By the time the slasher fights were finished and the pit scraped of blood and sanded fresh, Hoover had acquired two more friends by lending them a buck for barbecued chicken . . . two Umatilla Indians, one out of work from the harvest, offering us a generous gallon of cactus apple wine, and the other asleep in a dribbling wheelchair.

"Hee! Look at that," the one with the bottle said, indicating the mud puddle forming beneath the chair, "look what goes on. He cain do nothin' about it. Hey you, brother—wake up. You leakin'!" In a low voice he confided in me: "We aint real brothers;

we was together at the fishin' grounds on the Columbia before the government put the dam in, and in school some, and then in the War. We both was. He was a contender, you know, before the war. Look, his nose . . ."

He reached an enormous broken and swollen hand to his sleeping friend's nose and wobbled the nose about his face like a fat wart.

". . . no bone. They took the bone out for fightin'. Hee! Look that wheelchair leak! Funny thing he was doin' jus' that when it happened. I was right there. He stood up an' stretched in the foxhole an' started takin' a leak an' a chunk of somethin' they said come from a grenade catches him in the spine and lays him out. While he'uz leakin'. An' he been leakin' ever since."

The girls shook their heads in distaste at the crude tale, enjoying it; "Well, jeesus, the way you guyss *talk* . . .!"

The Indian was pleased. "You see *'Cross the Wide Missouri?*" he asked. "He was a chief in that. In Broken Arrow, too. A star, jus' like Jeff Chandler. He gets eight-five bucks a day jus' for his face, jus' for close-ups against the blue sky. Hey, wake up! Cock fight gonna start!"

He shook his brother until the sleeping face came to life—an incredible awakening of wrinkles: the sun coming up on the lava beds out of Sisters, the moving of ancient and myriad bark on the oldest Douglas Fir standing. He blinked at the dark mud in the dust beneath his chair and reached for the wine jug. Hoover took a sip and handed it to him.

"Whewie!" Hoover said, "What did you say that stuff was made of?"

"Cactus apples," the Indian told us happily. He took the jug from his brother in the wheelchair and gave him what was left of the barbecued chicken. "All prickly an' tough on the outside, sweet an' soft inside. Have some more. Pass it around."

Hoover had another taste and shook his head, then passed it on to me. It had a much higher alcohol content than regular wine, and it warmed me and cooled me at the same time. I thought it might ease my head but it only seemed to heighten the throbbing.

Wilson came walking from the shade and told us the fights were ready. "Let's get that chicken of yours killed and get a move on, Hoover. This is nothing but a bring-down out here. Arny and I have to drive back to the city tonight."

Carefully Hoover took the chicken from the car. It had stood calmly where I had left it. He sat on the ground holding the bird and leaned back against the car.

"Gotta be easy and not let 'em think you're nervous," he said. "They're right touchy."

"That's a lot of nonsense," Wilson said. "They don't have the brain to feel things like nervousness." No one answered him and he laughed. He pushed his hands in his pockets and walked back to the shade of the crabapples. ". . . brain about the size of a pea, clear down in their necks."

Hoover started tying the long, curved spikes over the bird's heels. Our group watched closely as the gaffs were lashed into place then covered with litle cloth holsters for safety until the fight started.

"Big White, huh?" the Indian said. "Never saw a white one fight before."

"Not many fight," Hoover said through the string he held in his mouth. "They got good endurance but most people think they're cowards, runners, so they don't give 'em a chance. Maybe they are cowards, I don't know. All I know is that this'n don't run from nothin'. Hell of a scrapper, only don't let on. Let them Filipinos think he's a runner an' we'll put the old shaft to 'em good, you get it?"

Everyone winked and nodded and drank on it. The girls beamed to be camp-followers of such an unusual bird, such a great cheeken. Hoover finished heeling the White and carried him to the pit where the other rooster was waiting. We all followed solemnly, boosters of the White. I pushed the wheelchair while the Indian with the bottle drank, then he pushed while I drank. The crowd greeted Hoover and his barnyard chicken with calls of derision. He grinned back at them: "Just for the barbecue, fellas . . . I tell you, that's all."

The chicken across the way struggled beneath the Filipino's arm. The bird's green and red feathers sparked like electricity. There were long scars on his shaved belly. "Umm," the Indian in the wheelchair said, speaking for the first time, "one hell of a bird, that Red."

Hoover showed his White to the laughter of the crowd, then gave it to me to hold while he took bets. He walked around the arena with a notepad, repeating, "White chicken, white chicken, give me odds." Everytime a spectator would shout "Red cheeken, twenty dolla," Hoover would write down the man's name and bet in the book. I held the chicken against my side, feeling its hot excitement vibrating against my ribs. I hardly knew what I was doing. I saw everything through my eyelashes. Hoover bet and covered until the crowd turned suddenly leery and refused to bet against the White anymore. He came to take the chicken and let me hold the notepad.

"Better stand out of the pit with the rest of our bunch, Arnold; sometimes steel goes to flying." He frowned at my sluggish movements. "Are you okay, boy?"

"Yeah."

"Sometimes people get a little squirmy watchin' a fight. You wanta wait outside with Wilson?"

"I'll be all right."

He steered me back to the rail where our group was. I closed my eyes and let the crowd noise wash past my ears, closing down the way Wilson had told me. I took a big swallow from the bottle when one of the girls put it in my hand. She took my arm and whispered, "I bet two dollars on heem. Real quiet. Hokay?"

I told her it was fine. Someone took the bottle away. It came back by again and I put it to my lips and swallowed gingerly. I could feel the cactus putting spines in my stomach. The girl beside me shook hard at my arm.

"Hey, *watch!* Watch our cheeken. What's the matter with you?"

Through my eyelashes I watched the referee draw the two handlers to the middle and let each chicken get four or five good pecks at the other's head as the men held the birds tight in their arms. The hackles flashed out. "You both ready?" the ref asked. Hoover nodded somberly. He backed off to his line. He knelt there, holding the White by the tail-feathers and whispering to him. The other man rubbed some kind of filthy ritual bag all over the Red's back and wings.

"Okay, okay, let's let 'er fly," Hoover said impatiently. The crowd laughed. Their derision reached my ears in a thin, soft string of words:—Big hurry to let him loose so you can chase him down, Hoover . . . better tie a string on him or you'll never see hide nor hair . . . he'll be long gone across the field . . . hey Hoover, hey now . . .

Hoover swallowed, constricting his neck much the way Wilson did. The White aimed its heat at the Red across the pit and dug long scores in the sand with his claws. The ref stepped back.

"Ready . . . pit your chickens!"

The men let go the tailfeathers and the birds charged across the sand. I could feel my lips drawn tautly back from my teeth. The air was hot coming across my tongue. Hell, hell, I repeated, blinking hard. The scratch of movement, the sun on the feathers, the spray of sand—all of it dashed against my eyeballs like scalding water, but I couldn't close them now. Fool, fool . . .

In the pit I saw the Red rise and kick and seem surprised to find the White fully as high in the air as he. They both fell back and advanced with more respect. "Kick the livin' Jesus outta him!" Hoover shouted. The White rose once more against the electric red blur of the other chicken and they fell locked together. "Aaaa . . ." the crowd said, no longer laughing. "Handle your birds," the ref said and he and the Filipino handler held the Red while Hoover extracted the White's long spike from its ribs. They moved back to their lines.

Hoover grinned and stroked his bird's darting head, while across the ten feet of sand the Filipino rubbed dust in the Red's wound to stop the bleeding. The ref counted the seconds. ". . . fifteen, sixteen, seventeen . . . Ready your chicken's . . . Pit 'em."

The birds clashed in the center once more. With a little effort I found that there were certain things to watch for, so I didn't have to take the crowd's word for a good hit. This time I was able to see the flash of the White's gaff as he sunk it into the red feathers. "God *damn*!" I shouted. "Handle your birds," the ref said.

"That White is one ringtailed son of a *bitch*!" the Indian with the bottle said, and we all drank to it.

The ref was scowling; he had money somewhere on that Red. The seconds he counted had a slow and bad taste to them. ". . . fifteen, sixteen, seventeen . . . Ready . . . Pit 'em."

This time the Red didn't try to match the White's incredible rise, but shuffled beneath the jump to safety. A wiser bird.—Wait 'im out, his handler had told him between rounds, don' try to match his jump; let him wear down.

The birds turned and the necks bobbled, beak to beak, near the ground. Cobrasnakes dancing, flames in the wind—they *couldn't* be chickens, just cruddy chickens. The White rose and spurred again but the older bird ran beneath him as easily as the last time. The next time he rose the Red was waiting for him on his back, slicing up with the gaff. I saw the blood spurt from the breast feathers, a narrow line, like a piece of red yarn clinging to the feathers. I felt the girl's hand tighten on mine.

I was yelling. "Handle 'em ref! They're hung!"

The ref scowled at me but ordered the chickens handled. Hoover took his bird and spit down its dry beak. He tried to press mud into the wound but the red yarn ravelled out, spreading on the feathers. "Bad hit," the Indian in the wheelchair said. He shook his head ominously and his great face rolled and rumbled.

"Ready . . . Pit your chickens."

The wound didn't bother the White's speed, but he knew better than to try to rise again. He circled and waited. Whenever the Red came too close the White speared for its eyes. They clashed again and the White sank both gaffs into the Red, and by the time they were parted he had the Red's left eye plucked clean and was holding it in his beak. "That bird won't play no more baseball in time to come," the Indian said.

Hoover handled the White and tried to stop the blood again by cauterizing it with a flaring matchhead, but the wound was too vital. It must have severed an artery clean. Hoover's blue overall legs were red and sticky from holding the chicken against him as he worked with him. At each break it seemed to be the White's gaff that had scored, but the Red only moved more stiffly and slowly and was cautious with his blind side. The Red bird was still strong; he didn't bleed.

Hoover cursed his chicken as he worked on it, calling it a "dirteatin' bastard" and a "Worthless leghorn." He spit water down its panting beak. He licked the dust from its eyes. He took its whole head in his mouth and breathed as if he were trying to breath his own life into it. Each time he gathered in his chicken at the break the bird was panting and beaten; its eyes were nearly closed and its dripping head lay limp on Hoover's pantleg. But by the time the twenty seconds were counted off and Hoover had finished administering his remedies the bird's head was high and ready once more, and its fierce blackspark eyes were searching across the ring for its ten-thousand year old enemy. The fighting periods became shorter and shorter as the fight went on, and there were more breaks. We finished our wine and yelled for Hoover and our chicken. The White continued to rally and meet the Red, but the Red, nearly blind, wounded in a dozen places, seemed to exist apart from life, seemed to have no actual life to risk—only flesh and eyes and bones.

The crowd sensed the White's last charge and edged up to honor it. Then men were screaming and rattling the rail with their hands. I felt those hands rattle in my head, like the dry clicking of hot grasshopper wings. My skull was coming apart at the forehead. "Bird! Bird!" I seemed to be shouting. I wondered briefly what had happened to Wilson, if he was shouting. I shook the rail. "C'mon bird, c'mon white bird!" Hoover reluctantly turned him loose; he knew the bird was through. In my wine high I watched the rooster float out of Hoover's arms in a slow, white and red arc, rising in the air this final time out of no force of muscle or tendon, but only because his veins now held only dust and the hot, dry air. He fell slowly toward the Red, light as a feather, and I saw him shimmer in the wine and the heat and the pain and felt my distorted perception climbing to an incredible pitch. I was seeing right through his feathers! I could see the intricate network of organs and tubes and dials pulsating inside his body . . . so many parts wiggling and working inside that little animal! And as he was drifting onto the Red's back I saw the pulsations stop and knew he was dead. I marvelled at the fact. I saw him *die*! I knew it before anyone else; I knew the *instant*.

"Aaaa," said the crowd when they saw the White fall from the Red's back. Even the heavy betters said no more; no cheering, just a long exhalation of breath: "Aaaaa."

My throat was raw with shouting and I felt a pain at my ankle. Dreamily I looked down at my leg; the Mexican girl was kicking me and shrieking: "Let go! You're busting eet! Let *go*!" I dropped her hand and took a deep breath. The other Mexican girl was cursing the loss of her two dollars. The Indian with the empty bottle looked sadly into it. From the wheelchair his brother shook his head at the soiled pile of red and white feathers on the sand: "One hell of a bird," he said.

"The dirteatin' bastard!" Hoover said and kicked his lifeless chicken across the pit. No one laughed at him. The winners approached him for payment of their bets, tentatively, not relishing their victory. As the men left the rail I caught sight of Wilson. He had moved from the crabapples and was sitting on a haybale in the shade of the burlap, where he had found it to his comfort. In contrast to all the flushed and excited faces around him, he remained dusty and cool.

Hoover paid the men from a great roll of bills, never questioning their claims or requests and refusing to look at the notepad I offered him. He peeled the money from his roll and fed it into any hand extended toward him. Occasionally he would look at the chicken and give it a good cursing. Wilson left his bale and came around the rail toward our group.

"Man, as soon as he finishes doling out that cash we're cutting back. We won't wait until tomorrow. It's too damned hot."

"Wait," I told him, "Wait a bit."

He looked irritable and puzzled. "What do you mean, wait? I thought you had a headache."

"I do have a headache, but let's just don't push . . ."

"And, God, it's such a drag, this oven. How can you get hung up with these smelly chickens? I never saw you get so hung up . . ."

Flaring, I told him I didn't know how and didn't give a damn! I couldn't help it. I couldn't break it. I don't give a damn, I insisted childishly.

He stared at me for a moment. I stood near him wanting to explain, feeling I should make an effort to show him how things were, why I couldn't help it, but he had turned away from me. He was watching the solemn paying of bets. The hidden wires pulled his lips into their grin. He shook his head at the people in bewildered amusement as they exchanged money somberly, reverently. ". . . over two or three bucks; Oh, the poor, poor dumb clods."

One of the women from the charcoal broilers moved slowly into the pit to pick up the dead White. I watched her easing toward the bird across the stained sand, strange and amorphic within the grey folds of her dress. She picked up the bird by one foot. "Hoover," I said, and Hoover dropped his roll of money and sprang to her.

"Here you! Hell's the matter with you? You think you're gonna cook up that bird why you're crazy as a coon. You leave him lay right where you got him. Drop him!"

Startled, the woman let the chicken fall back to the bloodly sand and hurried back outside, swishing her grey dress. Wilson put his hands on his hips and laughed at his brother's puzzling spread-legged stand over his dead bird; there was no malice or sarcasm in the laugh.

Hoover picked up the dead bird and tucked it under his arm while he gathered his money from the sand. The blood was beginning to dry and stiffen the once-white feathers—it was dry enough it didn't smear Hoover's shirt the way it had his pantslegs, but it was still sticky. "Dirteater," Hoover said while he finished his payments.

me now
e you
rtain
dont
ow me?

# POEMS, ETC.

Hsst. Over here. In the wings.
That puppet out on the apron, psht, pay him no
mind. *I* am the real me. I, here in the wings,
the secret observer and critic and director of not only
the puppet's gestures but of *yours* as well! And
now that I have your undivided attention there are a few
misconceptions I would like to set  .  .  .  huh  .  .  .  ?

H

b

Hst.
wing
the

Born full tilt into a river flowing—
choking, blinded by sight—into a torrent's
   roar,
   no chart to tell me of the torrent's going
   no record of a passing here before.

### Advise

This say I to every mind
who also is a head;
"Spend not so much time justifying . . .
and justify instead."

## Geometry

If you draw a line precisely safe and
parallel to mine
we can wail together clear on
past the stars
And never meet.
And since the holes between these
points of distant heat
Are deep and blind
Then sight a course for collision
and hang on tight  .  .  .
The precision in our yearnings is a lethal
kind.


## Geometry

If you draw a line precisely
Safe and parallel to mine
We can wail together clear on past the stars
And never meet.
Therefore: since—
The holes between these points of
distant heat
Are frozen blind, sight
A course for collision
And hang on tight—
Precision in our living is a
lethal kind.

what's happening *without judging* just reacting *respond* like blue produces blue not something like what's it mean I mean what the hell difference does it make what it means *you hear just the piece of groove under the needle—no more—if he'd wanted you figuring it out over there when you're way up here he'da put two needles on the thing now wouldn't he?* all right then. You don't never get something more'n what you pay for. And just like at any supermarket the more attention you pay—*before you step into this instant if you don't mind*—the more fly rides *fireworks* merry go rounds *rumbling earthquake comes* you get for your money. And, buddies, I can tell you for a fact. *It increases logarithmically!* fucking time but never let on. *Raskolnikov and the Police Inspector, separated by the roles they play, the rituals they are trapped in. Those roles and rituals can now be neutralized through the miracle of the total trip* on sale now

*but*

wait

*I hear hear that*

Listen—*hear it*

*that*

*that*

I get so I cannot remember the facts, just the feeling the facts set off.

I do not remember the names of the fish at the aquaruim.

I read Life's account of World War I and recall no places, dates, names, figures of incredible casualties, battles, who won or who lost socio-politics, geographical significance . . . only that:

"World War One was a bad fucking

Drag!!!"

I'm afraid if the world ever tests me on the lessons I should have learned, I will flunk out of this reality altogether.

What think you I care for the bloated dead agos when cherries are beginning to blossom (raining through)?

Or chomping ambush up the pike while I practice catching flies (thundering some, too)?

OR taking picture of your old lady's noisy black crow while it jabbers past. (thundering and—) OR (striking) lighting (JUMP!) Whew—missed—well, if you're gonna be a jap you gotta be fast

I like the surreptitious way this pen writes so ostentatiously.

Just noticing a thing about the tone of movies: there are certain unwritten and probably unconscious rules most of them follow. For instance, if the star in the picture is a criminal, and therefore due to come to a bad end, it is necessary somewhere about seven-eights of the way through the picture that he repent all his sins before god, his girl and, if at *all* possible without straining the plot too greatly, the second lead man who brings about the star's just destruction. This scene should take place with a church in the background (children, bell tolling, pretty girl with flowers), a saloon in the background (frightened townfolk beginning to creep timidly from behind watering troughs, swinging doors), or a police car idling in the background (siren sunk to a fluttering moan, light flashing, a fat, loveable fifty year-old char-woman running up the sidewalk with her apron flopping. "Joey! Joey!") And its always nice some dramatic clouds ya know, lotsa sidelighting, lotsa billow better use a filter to darken the sky; atta baby, that's the stuff . . . . okay team, here we go kiddies this one we play for keeps. Places. Crank it . . . . . . "

Errol Flynn staring over treetops at clouds; shoot from low, to one side: "I know this is going to sound silly . . . . but this morning, while I was hiding in that church . . . . . " Pull back, up, eyes drop: "I got this funny feeling . . . . . . "

I cut my wrists and bleed green ink, the drops drifting slow and soft as a green snow to the white meadow of my bedsheet . . . . .

Which recalls a bizarre occurrence: after a logics seminar in a hot, airless room—split varnish and dead flies on the window sills —I wait to speak with the professor. He smiles at my approach, splitting his chapped lips. As we talk a thin edge of blood, thin as a thread, surrounds his mouth. He doesn't notice the meager bleeding; he is not aware of my hypzotized stare: like many devout academicians his special field of interest is so hegemonic it blots out his students, his surroundings, his very physical body. He finishes answering my question and his eyes film over, the lips contract again into the pursed knothole of flesh leaving in my mind a faint after image of that red thread, describing a penciled smile on a clown's white face.

After All Night

The spring that drives me
has unwound,
the wind . . . . quieted;
And the night that hides me
look: ripped down!
where the peaks are clawing
lighted.

Placing a price tag before it is finished
May repeal the wage to be earned in the act;
The man who forges fantasies
and sets them free
makes more than by selling his fact.

Hold still you!
You've got experience. You're in top shape. You've been running the show for ten million years and no complaints so far.
There's no obligation but you have forged a *policy* out of the
scared sweat of nations and the policy holder never gets the *divi-
dends*. This last year alone you put on a payrole squeeze that alone
saved you from economic disaster. *Don't risk what you don't have
to!* The wise man guards his rear at all times.

(but darn it what about the faster tool?)
(do it . . . it has turned you thrice now from gained sewage.)
And one of the signals that comes through to one of the fanta-
sies (each other-place player would have, see, his *favorite* fan-
tasy to pull for), one of the hidden rules in this game of treasure
what is simply
*Make* (get the hammer and spike)
*My* (means the eye that's got)
*Self* (can't tell the players without programming)
*Comfortable* (cool everything)

197

# NORTHWEST REVIEW

**Editor**
Michael Strelow

**Fiction Editor**          **Poetry Editor**
Donald Bodey             John Ackerson


## Assistant Editors

**in Fiction**                **in Poetry**

Marilyn Desmond          John Addiego
Jay Goldstein            Cecelia Hagen
Christine McQuitty       Karen Locke
Ronald Renchler          Maxine Scates
                         Linda Schrevens
                         John Witte


## Advisory Editors

Kenneth O. Hanson
William Stafford
George Wickes

The **Northwest Review** is deeply grateful to the following individuals and institutions. Without them we would not be in print.

### Patrons
(\$100 or more per year)

Mrs. H. F. Cabell
Robert D. Clark
Mrs. Virginia Haseltine
Albert R. Kitzhaber
Mrs. Sidney Leiken
Glen Love
Mr. & Mrs. Carlisle Moore
Mr. & Mrs. Harold Schnitzer
Mrs. H. H. Strelow
Anonymous, New England
The Autzen Foundation
City of Eugene
Coordinating Council of
    Literary Magazines
Oregon Arts Commission
U. of O. Development Fund
U. of O. Friends of the Library

### Donors
(\$25 per year)

Mr. & Mrs. Roland Bartel
Mr. & Mrs. Edwin Bingham
Alice Henson Ernst
Mr. & Mrs. Otto J. Frohnmayer
Charles Gail
Walter Havighurst
Waldo F. McNeir
Mrs. Mary L. Merritt
John C. Sherwood
Leona E. Tyler
Anonymous

Contributions may be sent to the University of Oregon Development Fund designated for the **Northwest Review** and are tax deductible.

[This project is jointly sponsored by a grant from the Oregon Arts Commission and the National Endowment for the Arts, a Federal Agency created by an act of Congress, 1965]